About the author:

Sidney Edwards served in the RAF for 31 years, initially as a day fighter/ground attack pilot flying single-seat Hunter aircraft, and concluding his service as Group Captain, having been awarded the OBE, South Atlantic Medal and Queen's Commendation for Valuable Service in the Air. As well as the clandestine mission described in this book, Edwards completed several tours as a jet instructor, served as Air Attaché at the British Embassy in Madrid, and commanded advanced jet flying at the RAF Central Flying School, including the Red Arrows. His post-RAF career in civil aviation included being Managing Director of an air training college and ten years in key roles with easyJet. He lives in Letchworth, Hertfordshire.

MY SECRET FALKLANDS WAR

Sidney Edwards

Book Guild Publishing

Sussex, England

First published in Great Britain in 2014 by

The Book Guild Ltd
9 Priory Business Park
Wistow Road, Kibworth
Leicestershire, LE8 0RX
Freephone: 0800 999 2982
www.bookguild.co.uk
Email: info@bookguild.co.uk
Twitter: @bookguild

Typeset in Garamond

ISBN 978 1 909716 27 8

British Library Cataloguing in Publication Data.

A catalogue record for this book is available from the British Library.

To my wife Patricia, who died in December 2012, and to Ken Hayr, who was killed in an aircraft accident in June 2001.
Their incredible faith and support sustained me during the most difficult yet exhilarating period of my Royal Air Force career.

Chapter 1

'How long will it take you to get to Northwood?'

'About an hour, Sir.'

'Make it 45 minutes and I'll see you at the main gate; just follow my car in.'

'Yes, Sir.'

The caller was Air Vice-Marshal Ken Hayr, Assistant Chief of Air Staff, Operations (ACAS-OPS), in the Ministry of Defence, London. It was Easter Sunday, 11th April 1982, just over a week after Argentina's surprise invasion of the Falkland Islands. I was then a Wing Commander working in the Ministry of Defence Sales Organisation in another part of London and living in a small village near Marlow in Buckinghamshire. When Ken's call came through, I was mowing the lawn. RAF Northwood, north-west of London, was the Joint Force Headquarters for the operation to retake the Falklands.

I first met Ken Hayr when we joined the Royal Air Force together in 1954. He was a New Zealander and I was British. We trained as Flight Cadets on 'A' Squadron, Number 69 Entry at the RAF College, Cranwell. This was a three-year course, during which we completed officer training together and gained our pilots' wings on the Vampire jet aircraft. On graduation, Ken and I went to train as fighter pilots. We converted onto what was then the latest RAF jet fighter, the single-seat Hunter, at RAF Chivenor in Devon. This was a four-month course. We

1

thus knew each other very well as young men but after Chivenor were posted to different Fighter Squadrons and our paths crossed only occasionally during the rest of our RAF careers.

However, I had followed Ken's subsequent career with great interest because my fellow 69 Entry Flight Cadets and I had always predicted that Ken was destined for very high rank in the RAF. He was proving us right so far and along the way had gained a reputation as a tough but fair leader with a very determined streak. I knew that if Ken wanted me at Northwood in a hurry on a Sunday morning, there must have been a very good reason and I had better get my skates on. I left the mower in the middle of the lawn, rushed upstairs to change into uniform and drove to Northwood as fast as traffic and speed limits allowed.

I reached the main gate at Northwood 43 minutes after Ken's call, to find his staff car waiting. He waved and grinned at me from the back seat, indicating for me to follow, as the sentry opened the barrier and we drove through. After parking, we had time only for a quick exchange of salutes and a hearty handshake before we signed in at the entrance to the Headquarters. As we walked along the corridors, Ken apologised for spoiling my Sunday, saying that he would explain everything later but meanwhile we were expected at the briefing that was about to start. On entering the briefing room, I was impressed to see the large number of very high-ranking officers from all branches of the British armed forces. I recognised several of these distinguished military figures but I doubt if any of them recognised me! Apart from the Heads of the Royal Navy, Royal Marines, Army, Royal Air Force and Special Forces, there were many senior specialist officers from the operations, intelligence, engineering, medical and supply branches of all services.

There followed a comprehensive briefing on the current situation in the Falkland Islands, including the present and expected deployment of Argentine forces, not only in the Falklands but also in mainland Argentina. We heard that, while diplomatic efforts to persuade Argentina to leave the Falklands would continue, the Royal Navy had already prepared a Task Force that was sailing to the area. This action had three objectives. First, it would put pressure on Argentina by showing that we had the intention and the ability to recapture the Islands. Next, it would show the world in general and the Falkland Islanders in particular that we were not prepared to stand back and allow a military dictatorship to invade and occupy another country at will. Finally, and most importantly, if diplomatic pressure failed to dislodge the Argentine forces, it would give us the ability to carry out an amphibious assault, defeat the invaders and retake the Falklands. The briefing made clear that this would not be an easy operation. British forces would be operating at the end of an 8,000-mile supply chain in a very hostile environment, bearing in mind the extreme weather in the South Atlantic and the powerful opposing forces. The latter would have the considerable advantage of operating from their fixed home bases, with very short supply lines.

Conventional military thinking was that, in order to carry out a successful, opposed amphibious assault, an attacking force needed superiority in troop numbers of about three to one over the defenders. Given the time that Argentina would have to reinforce their troops on the Falklands while the Task Force sailed south, it was unlikely that we could achieve even parity in troop numbers.

On the contrary, we would almost certainly be outnumbered by perhaps three to one, with the British invasion force estimated at the time as about 3,000 troops against an estimated Argentine garrison of about 9,000. Furthermore, to ensure an acceptable chance of success, we would have to achieve command of the sea as well as air superiority. This all added up to quite a tall order.

After a briefing on the likely disposition of our forces when the Task Force was in position near the Falklands, the meeting opened for general discussion and clarification. At this stage, Ken Hayr asked me to stand. He introduced me, explaining that within a few days I would deploy to Chile on special, covert duties. He said that I would report directly to him but would be available through him to any other commander who needed special assistance, physical or intelligence, throughout the build-up to and during any subsequent hostilities. He explained that I was a former fighter pilot with experience in the air defence and ground attack roles, which would both be crucial once the fighting started, that I had diplomatic and intelligence experience, held a current high security clearance and was a fluent Spanish speaker. He added that, for good measure, I had attended courses at the RAF Staff College and the National Defence College, giving me a good grounding in joint force operations. As the assembled top brass looked me up and down, I imagined they would be thinking that I was probably some sort of Walter Mitty type who thought he could win the war single-handed. I felt that some of them might take up Ken's offer but only if they were desperate!

When the meeting finished, Ken took me aside to give me his ideas about the mission I was about to undertake. He explained that I had not been chosen for this special and important role merely because we were old friends, although he was sure that this would help a great deal in what he felt would become a relationship of complete trust and understanding. He said that I was selected because I held a convenient and unusual combination of experience, qualifications and personal qualities that the British Government was seeking in someone they wished to send to Chile to arrange with the Chilean Government for our Task Force to receive as much assistance as possible. I was also to remain in Chile to act as a direct, military link between the two countries.

Ken went on to explain that it would be for me to judge the diplomatic and military factors on the spot in Chile and make recommendations or take actions accordingly. He said that, although it made sense for me to base myself initially at the British Embassy in Santiago, to take advantage of the administrative support and secure communications available there, I would later have to decide if that would be the best arrangement. Although he could not predict what my precise role would be, Ken said that he knew it would be crucial during the battle to recapture the Falklands. He added that he knew he could rely on me. He explained that the Foreign Office was fully in agreement with my proposed deployment to Chile and that the British Ambassador in Santiago and the Chilean Ambassador in London were both in the picture.

Ken stressed the security aspect of my new role. He said that I should tell nobody where I was going or what I was going to do, not even my wife, Patricia. I should merely tell people that I was deploying on special duties until further notice. So that Patricia and I could exchange letters, he would arrange for us to use his PA in the

Ministry of Defence as a forwarding address. Ken also promised that he would telephone Patricia from time to time to let her know that I was fine. Finally, Ken asked me to attend his office in the Ministry of Defence in London early the next morning, to start two days of intensive briefings before flying out to Santiago. He said that he would speak to Air Vice-Marshal Alan Merriman, my boss in MOD Defence Sales, to apologise for stealing me at such short notice. I did not therefore need to attend my office until further notice.

I then left Northwood to drive home. It took considerably longer than 43 minutes to reach home, as I drove at a more leisurely pace than on the outward journey. On the way, I started to take in the enormity of the task I had just been given. I had never been to Chile nor, for that matter, anywhere else in South America and would be working virtually alone. However, I did not find it a daunting prospect. Rather, I found it extremely exciting. I also felt honoured and privileged that I had been trusted with the opportunity to play a part in this venture.

When I arrived home, Patricia was naturally desperate to discover what was going on. However, I explained that I could not give her any details other than that, following two days of briefings in London, I would be deploying on special duties until further notice. She accepted this without question. However, she said it was obvious to her that, with my background, this special duty probably involved the Argentine invasion of the Falklands in some way but that she would keep that idea to herself. I merely smiled.

Patricia was one of that wonderful, special breed of service wives who know and fully accept when they marry a member of the armed forces that this sort of thing can

Map of South America and the Falkland Islands showing the vast distances involved.

happen at any time. I knew that many thoughts and concerns would be running through her head but I also knew that she would not want to show any signs of this to me, so that I could concentrate on the task ahead. The love and support of my fantastic wife was to carry me through the most intensive, exciting and important period of my RAF service.

I changed out of uniform and finished mowing the lawn, but was 'mowing on auto-pilot' as I started to plan the next couple of days. I decided to spend the rest of the Sunday drawing up two lists: one for the domestic arrangements that Patricia and I would need to make for this unexpected and dramatic alteration to our life and one for the practical things that I would need to do before heading for South America. As we sat down to dinner, Patricia suggested that I leave everything on my domestic list to her, while I concentrated on the practical list. What a star!

Early the next morning, I reported to Ken Hayr's office. He jokingly thanked me for 'volunteering'. After a brief chat, during which he confirmed that I had no immediate problems or queries, he handed me a list of my appointments for the next two days. These included calls on our Chief of Air Staff, Air Chief Marshal Sir Michael Beetham, the Chilean Ambassador in London and his Air Attaché, staff on the South American Desk in the Foreign Office, the Director of Special Forces and senior officers on the Joint Intelligence and Operations Staffs in the Ministry of Defence.

One highlight of these briefings was when two members of the SAS collected me by car to take me to the London office of Brigadier Peter de la Billière, Director Special Forces. I had previously met Peter when his brother,

Commander Fred de la Billière and I were serving together at the British Embassy in Madrid, Fred as Naval Attaché and I as Air Attaché. Peter had visited his brother in Madrid, so I had met him socially. Peter was in uniform sitting at his desk. Unlike most military officers sitting at their desks in London at the time, he was armed. He was wearing two revolvers, one at each hip. Many terrorist organisations had the Special Forces in their sights and the capture or assassination of their Director would have been a great propaganda coup for any of these groups. I thought that Peter was therefore taking sensible precautions and wondered if he also had a pistol in a shoulder holster under his jacket – in his position I think I would have! Peter welcomed me warmly and after the usual pleasantries explained that, whilst he could not be specific at this early stage of planning, he was sure that Special Forces would be calling for my help at some time. He stressed that, to avoid compromising their operations, they would not be able to explain why they might need something done but that I could be sure it would be vital to their operations. I assured him that I fully accepted the need-to-know principle and would be very pleased to help at any time.

Another highlight of my briefing sessions was calling on the Chilean Ambassador in London, His Excellency Doctor Miguel Schweitzer and his Air Attaché, General Ramon Vega. We held an extremely cordial and interesting discussion, during which the Ambassador and General Vega assured me that I would receive a warm welcome in Santiago. They said that this referred not only to the officials I would meet but also to the general population. They also stressed that, within the bounds of the special diplomatic circumstances existing between Chile, Argentina and the UK, I could expect excellent cooperation from the Chilean armed forces in general and the Chilean Air Force in particular. I said that this was very welcome news as I had planned to start my time in Santiago with a call on General Fernando Matthei, Commander-in-Chief of the Chilean Air Force and member of the ruling military junta. General Vega said that this was an excellent idea as General Matthei had previously served as Air Attaché at the Chilean Embassy in London and was an Anglophile. He added with a smile that, like me, General Matthei was a Hunter pilot so we would have a lot to talk about. I congratulated General Vega on his excellent homework and the three of us had a good laugh about that.

We then had a most useful discussion about the Chilean and Argentine political and military scenes. The Ambassador and General Vega thanked me for my visit and wished me well for the future. I thanked them for seeing me at such short notice and said how grateful I was for their excellent advice. I left the Chilean Embassy in high spirits, feeling that I had made a good impression on Doctor Schweitzer and General Vega. I felt sure that the message they would undoubtedly send back to Santiago would be positive. I was also very happy with what they said about my likely reception in Santiago. I felt that this would make a solid foundation for my work there.

Chapter 2

The flight to Santiago took almost 24 hours. For obvious reasons, I had avoided the more direct route via Argentina, so there were several stops in the USA and South America. However, I had chosen a flight that would avoid a change of aircraft. En route, I tried to adapt to the five-hour time difference between Santiago and London by winding my watch back to Chilean time as soon as we were airborne from London and thereafter trying to sleep during the Chilean night, while remaining awake during their day. I also ate the size of meals appropriate to Chilean timings, regardless of what the cabin crew called them. I avoided alcohol and coffee.

For the first time, I now had the opportunity to muster my thoughts and plan my priorities on arrival in Chile. My flight was so far on time and due to arrive in Santiago just before noon the next day. I decided that, after a shower and change of clothing, I would pay courtesy calls on the British Ambassador and Defence Attaché the same afternoon. I would then seek an early meeting with General Matthei, as I believed him to be the key to any success I might be able to achieve in Chile. My reasoning was that he was not only the Commander-in-Chief of the Chilean Air Force but also a member of the ruling military junta. I therefore hoped that, with his Chilean Air Force hat on, he would be able to help us gain air superiority in the South Atlantic, an essential prerequisite to a successful

11

amphibious assault. At the same time, with his government hat on, I hoped that he would be able to gain us the necessary political backing, albeit covertly.

During my briefings in London, I had found our intelligence on Argentina's armed forces and their capabilities to be rather sketchy in several areas. As top priority, I therefore planned to ask General Matthei for as much cooperation over intelligence matters as possible. Closely allied to this, I would ask how far he was prepared to go in allowing our aircraft to use Chilean airspace or possibly even Chilean airfields, either in emergency or on a pre-planned basis. Finally, I planned to ask General Matthei how we might help Chile to strengthen its armed forces, since it was in our interest that Chile should maintain a strong military presence along its border with Argentina. This would force Argentina to keep an equally strong deployment of its forces tied up along the Chilean border and therefore not available in the battle for the Falklands. Argentina would consider this a sensible precaution against what they might think was Chile's intention to take advantage of Argentina's preoccupation with the Falklands to settle their long-running dispute over territory in the south of the continent.

As I finished my planning and settled down to sleep, I glanced up to the overhead locker where I had stowed my ceremonial sword with my hand baggage. I joked with myself that, if all else failed, I could use my sword to chase out the Argentine invaders. Although I intended to wear civilian clothes in Chile, I took uniforms, sword and aiguillettes in case the Chileans asked me to act as Air Attaché to cover my work there. In the event, I need not have taken my sword but the fact that I was allowed to carry it into the passenger cabin shows how far airport security has improved since then.

I awoke to find that we were flying down Chile between the Pacific Ocean and the Andes. From 40,000 feet, I was able to look down on the peaks of the mountains, covered in snow and regularly interspersed with extinct volcanoes. Many of the volcanoes contained frozen lakes. At the foot of the mountains, I could see the Atacama, one of the largest, hottest deserts in the world and reputedly the driest. This brought home to me that Chile was a country of contrasts.

On arrival at Santiago Airport, I found that our Defence Attaché had very kindly decided to meet me. Captain Malcolm Johns, RN, was of slight build and somewhat studious appearance. He was a very pleasant man who immediately made me feel welcome. Accompanying Malcolm was a Royal Naval Lieutenant, a member of the crew handing over the British warship HMS *Norfolk* and the Royal Fleet Auxiliary Tanker (RFA) *Tidepool,* which the Chilean Navy was buying from the British Ministry of Defence.

I had asked to be booked into a small hotel close to the Embassy. On the way, Malcolm suggested that I might like to use the remainder of the day to recover from the flight and start work the following morning. I politely declined and said that I had rested sufficiently during the flight, so would prefer to freshen up and change before calling on the Ambassador, followed by a meeting with General Matthei as soon as possible afterwards. Malcolm agreed to arrange this while I changed. He also kindly agreed to send Ken Hayr a short signal to say that I had arrived in one piece.

I was in the Ambassador's office in less than two hours. The Embassy was in a quiet, tree-lined avenue and occupied the top two floors of a multi-storied, modern building.

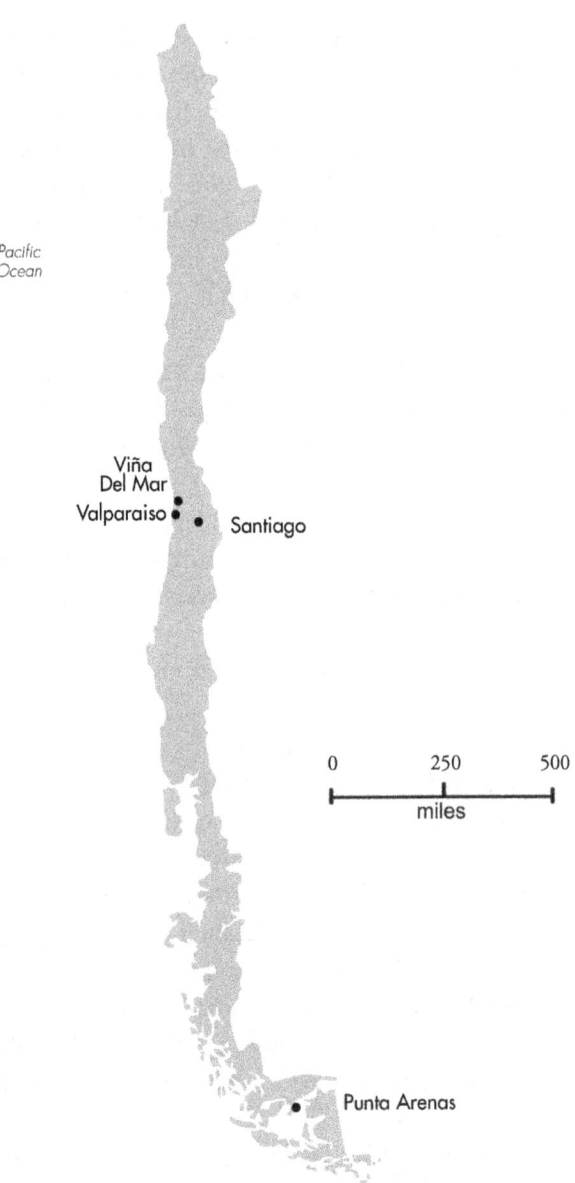

Map of Chile showing the long border with Argentina and the distance of
Punta Arenas from Santiago.

His Excellency Mr John Heath made me extremely welcome. He was a well-built, quietly-spoken man with an outwardly relaxed appearance. I soon discovered that this disguised a razor-sharp brain. He said that he had received a splendid report about me from Sir Anthony Acland. Sir Anthony was the Permanent Under Secretary, the senior civil service appointment, at the Foreign Office in London. He had served as the Ambassador in Madrid when I was Air Attaché, so we knew each other well. I admired, respected and liked Sir Anthony. We had got on extremely well together and I had never let him down during my three years in Madrid. For his part, Sir Anthony had always given me his complete support. That he had given John Heath such a good report on me was typical of Sir Anthony. I was extremely grateful to him for giving me such a good start in what might otherwise have proved to be a difficult relationship between John Heath and me.

John Heath said that he had 'done his bit' in World War II, so proposed to let me get on with the Falklands situation. (I later discovered that he had served with distinction as a Major in the Tank Corps). He said he knew from Sir Anthony that I had a good feel for diplomatic and political matters, that I would give good advice and take the right actions. He said he would continue to lead as normal a diplomatic life as possible while I got on with my work. In that way, he hoped to continue gleaning snippets of information that might help our cause. He authorised me to act as I saw fit and keep him in the picture only as and when I had the time or needed advice. He offered me the full cooperation and help of all members of the Embassy staff in Santiago. I was surprised and gratified that he was giving me such a free hand. This was a huge help to me at this early stage of my time in

Chile and I left his office feeling quietly confident about the future.

I next made a brief tour of the Embassy and met Mr Robert Gordon, First Secretary and Head of Chancery,

Santiago, the capital of Chile, situated in the middle of the country at the foot of the Andes mountain range.

Mr John Cummins, doubling as HM Consul and Embassy Administrative Officer, and the remainder of the staff present that afternoon. Everyone made me feel most welcome and offered their total support. I felt that this was a very good Embassy, with excellent staff, with whom I would be able to work easily. I was offered an office a few doors away from the Ambassador's.

Malcolm Johns had done an excellent job in arranging an appointment for me later the same afternoon with General Matthei in the Chilean Air Force Headquarters. I set off in good time to put the most important part of my plan into action. I had just enough time on the way to decide that Santiago was a more modern city than I had expected, with wide streets and tall, modern buildings in the centre. This was in marked contrast to the several areas of slums I had seen on the way in from the airport earlier that day.

When I arrived at the Chilean Air Force HQ, a Staff Officer met me at the entrance and escorted me straight to General Matthei's office. It was a very large room, which was just as well because the General had assembled what appeared to be every senior officer in his Air Force. I immediately recognised General Mario Lopez, the Head of Chilean Air Force Operations. Mario was the Chilean Air Attaché in Madrid at the same time as I was British Air Attaché. We got on very well in Madrid because, like me, he was a former Hunter pilot and we had exchanged many fond memories of our time flying that wonderful fighter aircraft in different parts of the world. The Hunter had been sold to many air forces around the world, including the Chilean Air Force, where it was still giving excellent service as a front-line fighter at the time of my arrival in Santiago.

17

Hunter aircraft were delivered to Santiago before the start of hostilities to boost the operational capability of the Chilean Air Force.

General Matthei shook me warmly by the hand. He made a short speech of welcome to the assembled officers and me before introducing me to them one by one. When we reached General Lopez, he gave me a warm Chilean 'abrazo'. (This is a sort of bear hug, while slapping each other quite fiercely on the back. Its use is confined to close friends and relations.) This did Mario Lopez and me no harm at all in the eyes of General Matthei and the others. General Matthei then said that he had assembled all of his senior officers to show them and me that we would all be working for a common cause and therefore needed to look each other in the eye. He offered full cooperation within the bounds of what was practical and diplomatically feasible. He stressed the need for secrecy and then handed the meeting over to me.

I thanked General Matthei and his senior staff for extending me the courtesy and honour of receiving me so soon after my arrival. I said I brought the greetings of Air Chief Marshal Sir Michael Beetham, Chief of Air Staff, Royal Air Force and handed General Matthei a letter of introduction that Sir Michael had given me in London. I stressed that, although at this early stage I could not confirm details, I was sure that our two countries would benefit from close cooperation to resolve the very serious situation developing in the South Atlantic. I explained that we all hoped diplomacy would persuade Argentina to abandon its foolhardy occupation of the Falklands. However, I confirmed that if this failed we would definitely invade and recapture the Islands. I then ran through what I had rehearsed during my flight to Santiago. I stressed that, although fully authorised by my Government, I was on a covert mission because we were well aware of the delicacy of relations between Chile and Argentina.

General Matthei replied that my remarks accorded with his own ideas. He repeated his earlier comment to his staff about the need for secrecy. After thanking me again for coming, General Matthei suggested that I should now liaise over details of our cooperation directly with General Vicente Rodriguez, Head of Chilean Air Force Intelligence. General Matthei stressed that he would be available to see me whenever possible but since, as a member of the military junta, he was also busy with government affairs, General Rodriguez had his full authority to work directly with me. He also offered me as my personal bodyguard, driver and Liaison Officer, Captain Patricio Perez, one of General Matthei's personal bodyguards. I told General Matthei that I was overwhelmed by his cooperation, generosity and thoughtfulness. General Matthei was a tall, very thoughtful man who spoke deliberately, with a slightly guttural Spanish accent, which I attributed to his Germanic ancestry. In spite of his position of power as one of the four most important figures in Chile, after President Pinochet, he had a relaxed and friendly manner and I took an instant liking to him.

During an interview many years later, General Matthei described this first meeting with me thus: 'Wing Commander Edwards did not appear to be in any way English. He was a young man, extremely active and displaying loads of adrenalin. He spoke perfect Spanish. He handed me a letter from the Chief of Air Staff of the Royal Air Force, giving Edwards full authority to negotiate with me over any matter in which we could cooperate. I found this very interesting.' In the same interview, General Matthei continued: 'After my meeting with Edwards, I spoke to General Pinochet. I told the President that through Edwards we had a great opportunity. It was not in our interest that Argentina should beat Britain because we knew that if Argentina was successful, we were next in line for attack. They had a long-standing dispute with us over territory in the south of our continent. Indeed, the Argentine President, General Leopoldo Galtieri, had said as much when addressing the crowd in Buenos Aires after the invasion, when he said that the Falklands were merely the start. He was talking just like Mussolini. General Pinochet agreed that I should work with the British, so long as this remained secret. We also agreed that we would not keep the Chilean Ministry of Foreign Affairs informed.'

After thanking General Matthei and the assembled officers cordially, I left with General Rodriguez and Captain Perez for a brief discussion about the way ahead. General Rodriguez and I agreed that Captain Perez would take me back to the British Embassy and collect me early the next morning to visit the Chilean Air Force Intelligence HQ. During the drive back to the Embassy, I reflected that I could not have wished for a better result from my first afternoon in Santiago. I had to remind myself that it was still only a few days since I had received Ken Hayr's telephone call, that 24 hours had been 'wasted' on my flight to Santiago, yet I had already been pledged the full support of the Ambassador and his staff, and the same from General Matthei. I was feeling tired but very satisfied as Patricio delivered me to the Embassy.

I had a brief discussion with the Ambassador to bring him up to date. John Heath congratulated me on hitting the ground running and I then settled down to compile a signal to Ken Hayr. Although I was now very tired, I knew that Ken would be anxious to know if his gamble in sending me out to Chile was likely to pay off. I was not prepared to make him wait until the next day for news. I wrote a long signal to Ken Hayr and handed it to the Embassy Duty Clerk for encryption and transmission to the Ministry of Defence in London. After confirming that the Duty Clerk had the telephone number of my hotel and my room number, I asked for a call if there were any urgent messages for me. Within half an hour, I was in bed in my hotel room. It was well after midnight and I immediately fell into a deep sleep.

Chapter 3

I awoke with a start to a loud ringing noise. Not having a clue where I was, I turned off the alarm clock before realising that the telephone was ringing. It was 3 o'clock in the morning. The Embassy Duty Clerk apologised for disturbing me and suggested I might like to return to the Embassy. I walked quickly through the deserted streets. I had forgotten that a curfew was enforced until 5 in the morning, which explained why the streets were empty. I was lucky not to be arrested or even shot by the Carabiñeros, as I had been warned that they could be rather trigger-happy. The Duty Clerk handed me several signals and I was delighted to see that one of them was from Ken Hayr. He thanked me for getting down to work so soon after my arrival and for the information in my first signal, which had been quite widely circulated around Whitehall. He sought clarification on a couple of points and asked me some supplementary questions. The other signals were from various departments in the Ministry of Defence, asking for extra information.

I drafted replies to all of these signals and handed them to the Duty Clerk one by one for encryption and transmission. Before I finished, more signals started coming in from London for me. I realised that, apart from Ken Hayr, many others in the Ministry of Defence saw the potential afforded by my direct link to General Matthei so I knew that I was going to be very busy. By the time

I had finished, the Embassy staff started to arrive for their normal day's work.

I immediately decided that I would need to move out of the hotel and into the Embassy in order to cope with the workload, the long hours I would have to work and the problem caused by the curfew. Having only just arrived, I had no idea if there was any accommodation available in the Embassy but was prepared to sleep in a chair for the next few days while I got on top of things. I sought John Cummins' help. I explained that, because of the workload, the time difference with London and the fact that the departments in the Ministry of Defence with which I would be in contact were on 24-hour manning, I needed to be available in the Embassy throughout the day and night. John was superb. He said that there were no bedrooms or bathrooms in the Embassy but he could provide me with a camp bed in my office. I said that would be splendid and asked if, as a temporary measure, I could wash and shave in the men's cloakroom late at night or early in the morning until I could get access to a shower. John said that was fine but he would work on arranging a shower!

Patricio Perez collected me on schedule to take me to the Chilean Air Force Intelligence HQ. He was in civilian clothes and driving a rather scruffy old Mercedes saloon, of which there were many in Santiago. He explained that this was to make us as inconspicuous as possible. He kept his pistol on the seat under his thigh, ready for action. Patricio was a slim, neat man with a small moustache; he was quietly spoken and in his late twenties. On arrival at the Chilean Air Force Intelligence HQ, we went to General Rodriguez's office. The General's secretary ushered us straight in. General Rodriguez leapt from behind his desk to shake me briskly by the hand. He was quite a large man who moved and spoke surprisingly quickly. I thought that he and I had probably cornered the market for adrenalin in the whole of South America. The General was enthusiastic about our cooperation. He explained that he was currently Chairman of the Chilean Joint Service Intelligence Committee, a post that rotated between the Chilean Navy, Army, Air Force and Carabiñeros. He described the Carabiñeros as a paramilitary police force, heavily armed and highly disciplined. He said that they were more like an army than a normal police force. I had already noticed as I moved around Santiago that the Carabiñeros wore very smart, army-style, khaki uniforms and were indeed more heavily armed than normal policemen. They also used armoured vehicles. Their importance in the country was underlined by the fact that the Head of the Carabiñeros, General Rodolfo Stange, was the fourth member of the military junta.

General Rodriguez said that, although he agreed with me that most of our work would involve the Chilean Air Force, we would have the full cooperation of the other Chilean forces through his position as Chairman of the Joint Intelligence Committee and via General Matthei. This was very good news that I knew would go down well in London. General Rodriguez gave me the answers to several of the questions I had received in the overnight signals from London. Those he could not answer immediately, he promised to resolve as soon as possible. He then took me on a tour of the building. He allowed me to see wall charts showing the disposition of Chilean and Argentine forces and encouraged me to talk freely to members of his staff. It was wonderful to feel such trust and I finished my tour with the impression that I was

25

already like an accepted member of General Rodriguez's staff. This feeling was reinforced when we returned to his office and the General told me that, to make life easier for me, he would issue me with a Chilean national identity card, driving licence and a pass exempting me from the curfew. Patricio arranged for me to have photographs taken and handed me all three documents before I left the building. My name was not a problem since Edwards was a relatively common name in Chile: there was even a bank called Banco A Edwards! I could see that there were some advantages to living in a military dictatorship, although I knew that many Chileans would not agree.

I left General Rodriguez agreeing that we would meet again the next day but that I could call him or visit him at any time at his office, home or anywhere else he happened to be, if it was urgent. He said that Patricio always knew where he was and would take me to him. I thanked General Rodriguez and left his office feeling that I would probably soon wake up to find that I had been dreaming.

As Patricio drove me back to the Embassy, I told him how impressed I was with General Rodriguez, his staff and the Intelligence HQ. I knew that this would get back to General Rodriguez and oil the wheels of our relationship but I also meant it as a genuine compliment. For his part, Patricio told me that everyone he had spoken to thought that I was doing a great job, especially bearing in mind the short time I had been in Santiago. En route, we called in at my hotel to pack my things and check out. I entered the Embassy feeling very happy about the way my second day's work was going but did not allow myself to think that it would always be like this.

In my absence, John Cummins had moved a camp bed,

a wardrobe and a cupboard into my office. John was already becoming one of my closest colleagues in Santiago. This was partly because of his no-nonsense, can-do attitude. This appealed to me because it matched my style of working. It was also because, although not part of his duties, John regularly put himself on night and weekend shift duties as Duty Clerk to share the burden on the small staff available at the Embassy during this crisis. In this role, John regularly encrypted and decoded signals between Ken Hayr and me. He thus knew exactly what I was doing, why I was doing it and how important it was. I came to rely completely on John during my time in Santiago and we became good friends.

As I was unpacking and stowing my things, John came into my office to see how I was getting on. He told me that I could use a shower in offices on one of the lower floors of the Embassy building and handed me a key. A Chilean company was using these offices but John, being John, had persuaded the owner to let me use the shower. To avoid revealing that someone was sleeping in the Embassy overnight, I believe he invented a cover story along the lines that he had a new member of staff, a fitness fanatic, who ran to and from the Embassy, so needed to clean up before changing for work. I thanked John sincerely for arranging yet another thing that would make my life so much easier.

I spent what was left of the evening composing and reading signals before settling into my camp bed for the night. I had to deal with several urgent items during the night, immediately showing the advantage of my new sleeping arrangement. The Duty Clerk could wake me, I could then slip on a robe, go to the Registry on the same floor a short distance away, deal with the signals and be back in bed again within minutes. I was lucky that I had always been able to fall asleep quite quickly. I was to become so short of rest during my time in Santiago that I could drop into a deep sleep even more quickly than usual.

The following day, Patricio arrived to take me to the Chilean Air Force Intelligence HQ again. However, he told me that General Matthei wanted to see me first, so en route he took me to the seat of government, Diego Portales. This was a large building about twenty stories high on Alameda, one of the main streets in Santiago. On arrival, Patricio drove into the basement car park and we took the lift to the top, where General Pinochet and the members of the junta had their offices. From the upper floors, there was an excellent view over Santiago with the snow-covered Andes towering in the background.

General Matthei saw me alone, while Patricio waited in the outer office. The General again welcomed me very warmly and explained that, although he had nothing specific to discuss, he wanted to ensure that I was receiving all the help I needed. I told him how much I appreciated his gesture in seeing me, said that everything was fitting into place and that I could not have wished for more cooperation from his staff. I made a point of mentioning how pleased I was with the excellent help I was receiving from General Rodriguez and Captain Perez. I was also able to pass on to General Matthei news I had just received that several Hunter fighter aircraft with spare parts were being prepared in England for delivery to Santiago as soon as possible. I also explained that we were identifying some more Hunters for later delivery and that a portable air defence radar and some surface-to-air missiles would be included in the package. General Matthei was very pleased to hear this, as the Chilean Air Force had been trying unsuccessfully for many years to obtain such equipment. Under the previous Labour Government there had been an embargo on the sale of military equipment to Chile and I knew from my time working in Ministry of Defence Sales that it took governments some time to overcome the inertia and change such policies. In thanking me for this good news, General Matthei said he welcomed the opportunity to strengthen Chile's air capability. As expected, Peru was siding with Argentina over its dispute with Britain and would no doubt be looking for any opportunity to take advantage of Chile's difficulty in protecting its northern border with Peru at the same time as its southern border with Argentina, bearing in mind the huge distance between them.

(On a dark night shortly afterwards, I went with General Rodriguez and Captain Perez to the military part of Santiago airport to watch six Hunter aircraft and many spare parts unloaded from a Boeing 747 cargo aircraft. These were followed shortly afterwards by surface-to-air missiles and a portable radar set.) General Matthei and I also discussed their very generous and much appreciated offer to allow us to delay the handover to the Chilean Navy of HMS *Norfolk* and RFA *Tidepool*, should we wish to use them in our Task Force. In the event, we politely declined the offer to keep HMS *Norfolk* because the small RN handover crew and the type of equipment aboard *Norfolk* made it unsuitable for rapid deployment. Warships entering a combat zone needed to have up-to-date equipment and weapons systems, while their crews needed to be fully worked-up and operationally ready. However, we accepted the offer to retain RFA *Tidepool*, which subsequently joined the Task Force and played an important part in the

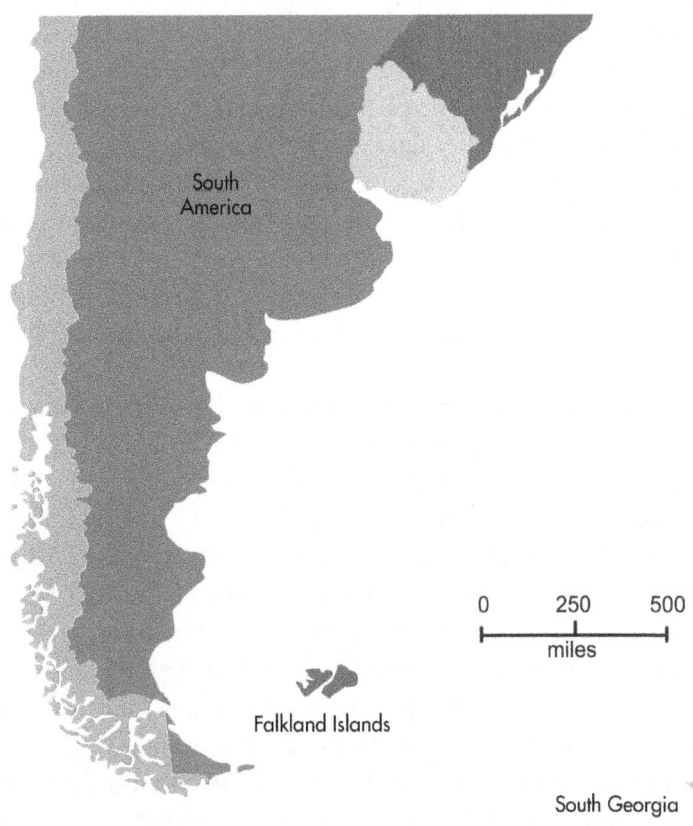

The first action of the Falklands War occurred when South Georgia was recaptured from the occupying Argentine forces.

operation to recover South Georgia. It then joined the main Task Force for the remainder of the war.

As I left General Matthei's office, he reminded me that I should feel free to visit him whenever I felt the need. As General Rodriguez had previously done, General Matthei said that Patricio always knew how to find him.

As Patricio and I were driving to the Chilean Air Force Intelligence HQ, I noticed that his pistol had moved on the seat under his thigh so that the barrel instead of the butt was pointing in my direction. I joked with him that he risked castrating me if the safety catch slipped off and that I preferred the previous arrangement whereby the barrel was pointing at his family jewels. We laughed about it but he did not let it happen again because we both knew that he would not be able to use his pistol as quickly with the butt under his leg. Later that day, when I was in his office, General Rodriguez opened a briefcase that was on the corner of his desk to remove some papers. Unfortunately, it then slipped off his desk and landed on the floor with a loud bang before either of us could stop it. Most of the contents fell out all over the floor. Three hand grenades rolled across the room and a pistol with two spare clips of ammunition bounced onto the carpet. There were also papers everywhere. The General swore profusely and we both knelt down to collect everything and stuff it back into the briefcase. He then apologised but I said there was no harm done because at least the pins were still in the grenades and the pistol safety catch was on. However, I remember thinking that, even if the Argentines failed to find me and bump me off, Patricio or General Rodriguez might manage to do the job accidentally on their behalf.

Chapter 4

I now entered a period lasting just a few days during which I consolidated my position as a cuckoo in two nests, one in the British Embassy and the other in the Chilean Air Force Intelligence HQ. Such was the quality of my acceptance into both communities that I felt as though I had been in both nests for several months, rather than only a few days. In the Embassy, on the practical side, I was never short of offers of typing, cups of tea, coffee, soft drinks, food or just 'is there anything I can do to help?' On the professional side, everyone from the Ambassador down gave me excellent briefings or advice whenever needed and nobody ever refused to see me as soon as I asked. I could not have asked for better cooperation from my new colleagues there.

During this period, an amusing incident occurred in the Embassy very early one morning. Having finished my customary shower, I was on my way back up to the office when the lift stopped at an intermediate floor. A young lady I had never met before entered the lift, went up two floors with me and then got out. We exchanged the usual remarks about the weather, how early in the morning it was, etc, before I continued my ascent alone. We acted as though it was an everyday occurrence for a chap with wet hair to be in the lift of an office building, wearing a robe, clutching a toilet bag and with a bath towel over his shoulder. I never saw her again.

At the Chilean Air Force Intelligence HQ, it seemed to me as if they were trying to outdo the Embassy. The courtesy and hospitality of the staff were superb. I quickly achieved a wonderful working and personal relationship with members of the Chilean Air Force and, although we remained utterly professional, we enjoyed plenty of jokes together, usually at the expense of Argentina. I have always maintained that, no matter how serious the work, one should always allow time for a little humour to relieve the tension. This appealed to the Chileans and I soon discovered that they had an excellent sense of humour. I quickly became known to my face as 'El Gringo Loco' (The Crazy Englishman), which I took as a sign that I had been accepted into their group.

No subject was off-limits with my new Chilean colleagues. I was very interested to hear their description of the military coup that had brought President Pinochet to power. They told me that the previous Communist Government under President Allende was inefficient and extremely corrupt. They gave examples of extreme shortages in the shops of basic commodities such as bread, while government officials and senior Communist Party members were receiving unlimited deliveries of all types of food and other luxuries at their houses. They had found this particularly galling when they had to queue very early in the morning in the hope of buying bread and other basic items.

Apparently, wages were so poor that Air Force officers to whom I spoke had to supplement their salary by driving taxis or working as waiters. It seemed to me that it would have been wise for any government to keep the armed forces reasonably well paid. This was especially true in South America, where I reckoned that there were probably degree courses in how to mount a military coup.

One officer, who was a Hunter pilot at the time of the coup, described how he was flying over Santiago with other Hunter aircraft as General Pinochet's tanks were rumbling into the city. At the time, President Allende was in the Moneda Palace in Santiago, wondering whether the Air Force would join Pinochet's coup. This pilot received orders to give a convincing firepower demonstration to persuade Allende to surrender, so he blew in the front doors of the Palace with a salvo of well-aimed rockets. This had the desired effect and was a key point in the successful overthrow of the communist regime. I considered this to have been an excellent example of the judicious use of air power.

A few days after my arrival in Santiago, Patricia's first letter arrived in the diplomatic bag via Ken Hayr's PA. It was wonderful to get news from home and Patricia continued to send me one or two letters each week during my absence. I also always made time to write back to her at least once per week. I found that the times when I was either reading Patricia's letters or writing to her were very special moments in an otherwise extremely hectic life. That I was thus regularly able to move mentally from Santiago to the Thames Valley was very therapeutic and that helped me considerably in the demanding work I was now doing. It was also a great comfort to me to read regularly in Patricia's letters that Ken Hayr had just telephoned her to say that he had just heard from me, that I was well and had sent her my love. Of course, I never mentioned Patricia in official signals to Ken but he knew that his little white lie was important in the special circumstances of our enforced separation. I thought that Ken Hayr was not just a great leader but also a very kind and thoughtful man. I decided that I would do anything for a man like that.

35

During this early period in Santiago, I decided that it was very important to take care of my health because I had no idea how long I would be working single-handed on my special duties and was already getting quite short of sleep. I started to take short naps whenever possible during the day. I let my colleagues in the Embassy and the Chilean Air Force know about this so that they would not be surprised if they found me nodding off in a chair, a car or an aircraft whenever there was nothing urgent to occupy me. I would often ask a colleague to wake me in, say, ten minutes or whenever something important happened. As a result, at other times I was able to remain awake for long periods when necessary.

So far as exercise was concerned, I could not afford the time to visit a gym or go jogging so I used stairs instead of a lift whenever possible and carried out a daily fitness routine in my office. I also considered it important to eat regularly and sensibly. There was an excellent Argentine restaurant opposite the Embassy that the staff used regularly. I decided that it might appear suspicious if a new member of staff never used it so I occasionally took a light lunch or supper there. Also, like other members of the Embassy staff, I occasionally ordered a steak sandwich to be sent over if I was too busy to take a proper meal. As in any public place, we avoided talking about our work in this Argentine restaurant, but our relationship with the staff there was always polite and courteous. This remained the case even at the height of the war, when our fellow countrymen were killing and maiming each other during what turned out to be an extremely bloody conflict. The irony of this situation sometimes struck me when eating an Argentine meal washed down with a glass of that country's excellent wine, listening to Argentine background music.

Similarly, there were several restaurants near the Chilean Air Force Intelligence HQ. I would sometimes take lunch or supper at one of those. General Rodriguez or Captain Perez would accompany me whenever possible when I was eating out, so that I was never short of company or a bodyguard. On a few occasions, when neither was available, they would suggest that someone else should accompany me; this was normally a male officer.

However, on one such occasion, they suggested that General Rodriguez's secretary, Vicky, could accompany me to lunch, as there was nobody else available. Vicky was a very attractive lady in her late twenties, with whom any man would have been delighted to take lunch. I said that I would be pleased to take lunch with Vicky but wondered what she or her boyfriend would feel about that. General Rodriguez told me that Vicky was a willing volunteer and that, to avoid any misunderstandings, she had already told her boyfriend. He added that, in case I had any doubts about her ability as a bodyguard, she was armed, had trained on the same course as my own bodyguard, Captain Perez, and was an experienced protection officer. I enjoyed a particularly pleasant lunch with Vicky that day and we got on very well. Of course, we already knew each other through my frequent visits to General Rodriguez's office but this was the first contact I had with her in an informal setting. She was very intelligent, with a wide range of interests and an excellent sense of humour. She was delightful company and for an hour I was able to relax and put the very serious nature of my work to the back of my mind.

Chapter 5

My top priority was to help the Task Force to achieve air superiority. I knew that our very small number of air defence Sea Harriers would be hopelessly outnumbered by the much larger fleet of Argentine combat aircraft. These Skyhawks, Mirages, Super Etendards, Canberras, Aeramacchis and Pucaras represented a formidable threat. Any that penetrated our air defences would be able to cause deadly damage not only to our ships but also to our troops and equipment once they were ashore. We would of course be at our most vulnerable during the landing phase of the operation to retake the Falklands.

Whilst some air defence radars were available within the Task Force, we had no high-level, airborne early-warning aircraft to give us the long-range warning of attacking aircraft that would enable us to intercept them well before they could attack our forces at sea or on the ground. The alternative of mounting extensive combat air patrols was very expensive in terms of pilot fatigue, fuel consumption and expenditure of airframe or engine hours. It would be possible to mount only a limited number of combat air patrols.

The Chilean Air Force was operating a long-range radar on a mountain near Punta Arenas at the southern tip of Chile. I discovered that from there it was possible to obtain good radar cover of Argentine air movements around the airfields at Ushuaia, Rio Gallegos, Rio Grande, and

Map of Southern Chile and Argentina showing the strategic importance of Punta Arenas in relation to the Falkland Islands and the main military bases in southern Argentina.

Comodoro Rivadavia. Since these were the most likely bases from which Argentina would mount attacks on British forces, General Rodriguez and I agreed that we would devise a system to make this information readily available to the Task Force.

Using this radar, the Chilean Air Force could immediately identify the height, direction, speed and numbers of Argentine aircraft leaving these bases in southern Argentina. General Rodriguez readily agreed that this crucial information would be passed rapidly by secure link to the Chilean Air Force Intelligence HQ in Santiago, where it would be at my disposal. General Rodriguez and I discovered that we could improve radar cover in the area by installing another radar near the border with Argentina. I decided to investigate whether there was a portable radar set available from British resources. I immediately sent a signal containing this most welcome information to Ken Hayr back in London, asking how we could pass it to the Task Force. I also asked Ken if he could send us a portable radar set.

Ken reacted with his customary alacrity. He replied that he was delighted at this turn of events and would dispatch a portable radar set as soon as possible. He also arranged for a team of four SAS men to fly to Santiago with a secure Satellite Communications System (SATCOM). They arrived within a couple of days, by which time General Rodriguez had agreed that we could base them in the Chilean Air Force Intelligence HQ. Thus, these vital radar plots could be passed securely and speedily to the Task Force, giving maximum possible notice of impending air attacks. This team was also able to pass on to British forces other information available within the Chilean Air Force Intelligence HQ. They installed their small SATCOM aerial inconspicuously among the many other aerials that the Chileans already had on the roof of this building. A few days later, the portable radar set arrived by air for installation in southern Chile, to supplement the cover provided by the Chilean Air Force radar at Punta Arenas.

We accommodated the SAS team in a bungalow in a quiet suburb of Santiago. They worked in shifts so that we had continuous cover in the Chilean Air Force Intelligence HQ throughout the war. There can be no doubt that, without the timely information this team passed to the Task Force, we would have suffered many more losses to enemy air action and would almost certainly have lost the war. This was a prime example of the important intelligence-gathering role that the SAS plays. Apart from anything else we achieved through cooperation with our Chilean colleagues, this result fully justified the decision to send me to Chile. I was thrilled and privileged to have played a part in this episode because I knew how much it meant to those responsible for the air defence of our forces and especially to our Harrier pilots, who thus received accurate and timely information about enemy air activity. Of course, as subsequent events proved, this did not prevent Argentine aircraft from often penetrating our defences and sometimes causing serious damage. Our defending force of Sea Harriers, surface-to-air missiles and anti-aircraft guns was not large enough to cope with mass raids. However, this information allowed the Task Force to allocate our slim resources most effectively to reduce the impact of each attack

I kept a tally of Argentine aircraft destroyed against British surface ships sunk or badly damaged and at one stage it seemed to me that we were trading on a one-for-one basis. I realised that we could not continue at this rate of attrition. Apart from the human tragedy in terms of lives lost and personnel wounded, I was worried that we might run out of warships before Argentina ran out of aircraft. However, we continued to pass all radar information to the Task Force and the balance of losses started to swing in our favour.

In discussions with my Chilean Air Force colleagues, we agreed that the Argentine pilots were showing great courage in setting out on their attack missions knowing that there was a very high probability that they would be shot down and killed or captured. We also thought that they showed great skill and bravery in pressing home their attacks at low level over the sea, short of fuel and hundreds of miles from their own bases.

When I explained to General Rodriguez how vital this information was proving to be, he assured me that the Chileans would do their utmost to keep their radar operating day and night to help our war effort. He added that they intended to delay routine servicing of the equipment as long as possible. As a result, there was only one brief period during the war when radar cover was not available due to equipment breakdown. By sad coincidence, it was during this period that Argentine aircraft carried out their devastating attacks on our ships as they unloaded troops and equipment. The Welsh Guards bore the brunt of this attack, which left the landing ship *Sir Galahad* in flames and damaged beyond repair. The landing ship *Sir Tristram* was also hit by bombs although she was repairable. Thirty-nine Welsh Guardsmen were killed during this attack as well as ten other men. A further 115 personnel were wounded. This incident sadly demonstrated the deadly effects of enemy air attacks and made General Rodriguez and me even more determined to provide the Task Force with as much advance warning of air raids as possible. It also showed how vulnerable the Task Force would have been throughout the war had this vital information not been available.

Chapter 6

'Please nip out to San Felix Island as soon as possible and report on its suitability for Nimrod operations,' said the signal. This was a typical request from Ken Hayr. It was the result of a previous discussion I had with General Rodriguez about the possibility of using a Chilean airfield to launch sorties with Nimrod Electronic Intelligence-gathering (ELINT) aircraft. The object was to fly at high level along the Chilean border and out into the South Atlantic, collecting important electronic information. General Rodriguez had said that they were very happy to help but, in order to keep the operation secret, as well as for political reasons, they would initially prefer us not to use a base on the Chilean mainland. However, he thought that San Felix Island might be suitable and General Matthei would be happy for us to use this if it was. San Felix Island was a remote Chilean possession some 700 miles out into the Pacific Ocean from the Chilean port of Valparaiso.

A short while after I received Ken's signal, General Rodriguez and I took off in darkness from the Chilean Naval Airbase outside Valparaiso. We were in a light, twin-engined communications aircraft of the Chilean Navy with Commander Pedro Anguita at the controls. Pedro was the Chief of Staff of the Chilean Naval Air Service. Apart from Commander Anguita and General Matthei, only Admiral Tobino Merino, Commander-in-Chief of the

45

Chilean Navy and member of the military junta, knew where we were going and why. The Commander of the Chilean Naval Base on San Felix Island knew only to expect an aircraft. Pedro had decided to do this job himself in order to keep the number of people involved to the minimum. Since it would take several hours for our propeller-driven aircraft to reach San Felix Island, General Rodriguez and I took it in turns to sit on the flight deck to keep Pedro company (and awake!) while the other brought coffee and snacks onto the flight deck or took the opportunity to doze in the back.

When dawn broke, we were well out into the Pacific with no land, shipping or other aircraft in sight. We droned on for another couple of hours with nothing but blue sky above and equally blue sea below before a small dot appeared on the horizon. As the dot slowly grew bigger, we could make out the shape of San Felix Island. It was a very small island made of jagged, volcanic rock. There was a single runway extending almost the entire length of the island, with a taxiway leading to a small parking area to one side of the runway. At the side of the parking area there were several buildings and a control tower. From the air there appeared to be nothing else on the island and there was certainly no other sign of human habitation. I told my two companions that this looked to me like an excellent location for a James Bond film. General Rodriguez laughed and said that I would find my words even more appropriate when I had inspected everything.

As we prepared to land, I was able to take good note of the approaches to both ends of the runway. There was no room for error, since there were jagged rocks close to both runway thresholds and the ground then fell away steeply to the sea below. Pedro made an excellent approach and landing and we were soon coming to a halt on the parking area, where a small reception party was waiting for us. The Chilean Naval Base Commander and his staff made us very welcome. He told me that he had been instructed by his Commander-in-Chief, Admiral Merino, to show me all the facilities on San Felix Island, answer all my questions and give me any assistance I needed. He then took us into his office alone, where I was able to give him in strict confidence an idea of what I needed.

Without naming the Nimrod at this stage, I explained that Admiral Merino had given us authority in principle to base a large RAF aircraft on San Felix for a short while to mount long-range sorties at night. I explained that my job was to check whether San Felix was suitable to operate this aircraft safely. My first priority was to check the surfaces of the runway, taxiways, parking area and their surrounds for any loose articles or material that could be ingested through Nimrod's air intakes, causing irreparable damage to the engines and preventing these important missions from going ahead. I did this by walking the whole way, carefully scanning the ground. I found that the Chilean Navy's housekeeping in this respect was excellent and all of these areas were clean.

The Nimrod was a heavy aircraft so I next checked the load-bearing qualities of these surfaces. My hosts told me that the sub-surface was volcanic rock and the figures they gave me for the load classification numbers for each area bore this out. I did not think that this would cause any problems but made a note of the numbers to pass to Ken Hayr. Nimrod was not particularly high off the ground and I knew that this version of the aircraft could have a variety of modifications fitted beneath its wings, so I was

47

careful to check the areas to each side of the runway and taxiways to measure the height of any objects that would come underneath Nimrod's overhanging wings. Finally, I checked the runway gradient and the braking action for dry and wet runways. I also obtained statistics for the prevailing surface winds and other meteorological factors. Because I knew that Nimrod would be operating mainly at night, I was careful to make a note of all runway and airfield lighting. Subject to what Ken Hayr and his staff thought, I believed that Nimrod could operate safely from San Felix Island when lightly laden but that it might be marginal if the aircraft were heavily laden. I now turned my attention to matters of administration and logistics.

There was only a small quantity of jet aviation fuel available on the island and I estimated that Nimrod would swallow this at one gulp. I also believed that, because of the restricted runway, the Nimrod Captain would wish to take off and land with minimum fuel on board when operating from San Felix. In discussion with General Rodriguez, we decided that the only solution would be for us to arrange for C130 aircraft of the Chilean Air Force to airlift extra fuel in 50-gallon drums onto the island, assisted by Royal Air Force C130s, if I could arrange this via Ken Hayr. Even then, we calculated that Nimrod would need to refuel on the Chilean mainland in order to fly long-range missions into the South Atlantic. General Rodriguez agreed to look into this immediately while I continued checking on other administrative details with the Base Commander.

I learned that the Chilean Navy crewed San Felix Island rather as one would operate a lighthouse or oil-rig. Two crews operated on a month-on, month-off basis. There was sufficient spare accommodation and messing available for our Nimrod crew (without giving the game away, I had asked for facilities for up to twenty men). The Base Commander assured me that, to maintain the security of our operations, he would not rotate his current crew until our operations had finished, would brief his crew on the need for security and would censor all mail. He added that outgoing telephone calls were already tightly restricted but he would also monitor them strictly to avoid any leaks. He was fully confident that his 'ship' would not have any leaks.

At this stage, General Rodriguez reappeared with a satisfied smile on his face and took me to one side. He explained that he had spoken by secure link to General Matthei, who had suggested that we might like to use Concepción to refuel Nimrod at night. Concepción was eminently suitable for our Nimrod operations. On the coast some 300 miles from Santiago, the Carabiñeros would be able to restrict public access to the airport and the surrounding area while Nimrod slipped in and out during the hours of darkness. We therefore had a plan that I knew Ken Hayr would jump at. Nimrod could use San Felix as an operating base, landing and taking off with low fuel loads, which would make its operations much safer on the restricted runway there. It could then stage through Concepción in darkness to take on a full fuel load and fly its missions out into the South Atlantic, recovering to San Felix Island with minimal fuel load at the end of its sorties.

General Rodriguez and I then rejoined the Base Commander to complete the last part of my inspection of the facilities on San Felix. As we climbed into a vehicle, General Rodriguez reminded me of the remark I had made when we flew onto the island that this looked like an

49

ideal location for a James Bond film. He said that I would now see how true that remark was. We drove to the other side of the island, well away from the runway, to an outcrop of rocks. As we approached, I could see a gap in the rocks, within which was an opening to a cave. We left the vehicle and walked through the gap into the cave entrance. Descending a wide stone staircase cut into the wall of the cave, we soon entered a huge cavern and looked down on a James Bond-style underground harbour.

There was a deep-water passage from the open sea leading to a quay with moorings for several surface vessels or submarines. This harbour was fitted with the usual equipment of a naval base, including refuelling and storage facilities, workshops, cranes, various buildings and floodlights. Nothing was visible from the air and the thickness of rock in the roof gave excellent protection from aerial attack. I told General Rodriguez and the Base Commander how impressed I was with this facility and joked with General Rodriguez that I thought he was a greater fan of James Bond than I was. In the serious discussion that followed, my two hosts thought that, subject to checking with their respective chiefs, we might find this particular asset quite useful.

By the time we returned to the other side of the island, it was getting dark. Our pilot, Pedro Anguita, had sensibly taken the opportunity to get some sleep in preparation for our long flight back to the mainland and was now waiting on board for us. After thanking the Base Commander and some of his senior staff who had come to see us off, we departed into the now starlit night. As we did during the outward flight, General Rodriguez and I took turns on the flight deck with Pedro. During my spells in the back, I composed a long signal for Ken Hayr, describing all I had seen and discussed on San Felix Island. I handed this to the Duty Clerk for encryption when I finally returned to the Embassy in Santiago in the small hours of the following morning.

Chapter 7

The reaction from London was positive and rapid. A few days later, the RAF sent a Nimrod ELINT aircraft from the UK to San Felix Island, where it landed without incident. At the same time a C130 Hercules in RAF markings arrived at Easter Island, a Chilean possession way out in the Pacific, where it was repainted overnight in Chilean Air Force markings. It then proceeded to the Chilean mainland to help ferry fuel and other supplies to San Felix Island in support of Nimrod operations.

For the first Nimrod flight from San Felix Island to the mainland for refuelling, General Rodriguez, Captain Perez and I flew from Santiago to Concepción to satisfy

C130 Hercules Aircraft. The RAF flew several of this type of aircraft inside Chile during the war. They were flown to Easter Island to be painted in Chilean Air Force markings before flying to mainland Chile to carry out important support and supply missions.

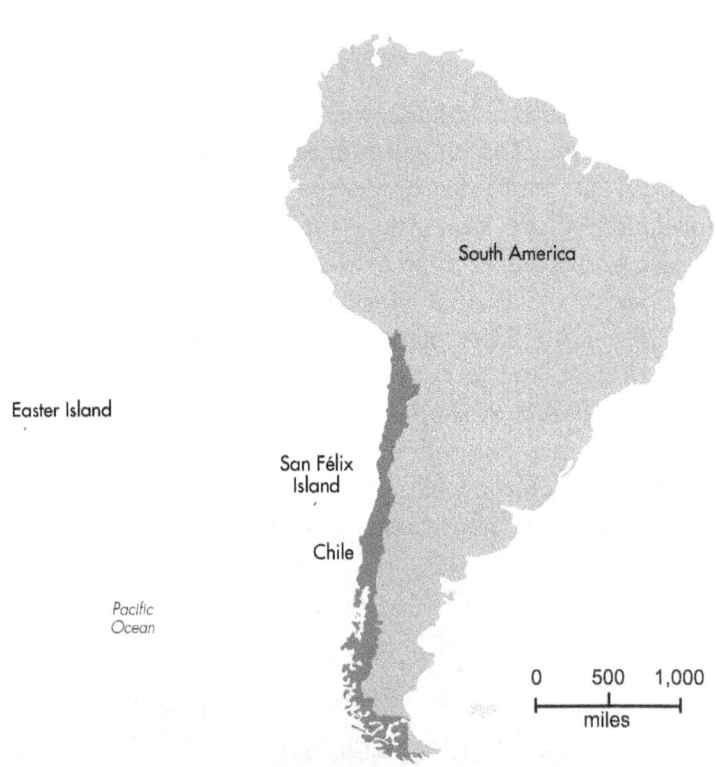

RAF aircraft operating in Chile during the war staged through Easter Island, a Chilean possession way out in the Pacific Ocean.

ourselves that the arrangements we had requested were satisfactory. It was reassuring to find that we had to pass several Carabiñero checkpoints on the way and that access to the airport itself was strictly controlled. Shortly after our arrival, Nimrod descended out of the night sky and taxied onto the ramp in front of us. Even at close quarters it was difficult to tell that this was a British military aircraft. The RAF roundels were discreetly marked on the fuselage and wings, which were painted in a neutral colour, with no camouflage. It had been developed from the original Comet civilian passenger aircraft so there were windows all along the fuselage. This aircraft could easily have been mistaken for a civilian passenger or freight aircraft dropping into Concepción for a refuelling stop.

While the aircraft was receiving a full load of fuel, General Rodriguez and I went on board to speak to the

During the early part of the war, the RAF operated a Nimrod aircraft from San Felix Island in the Pacific Ocean and Concepción on the coast of mainland Chile to gather electronic intelligence. It flew missions at high altitude along the border between Chile and Argentina and out into the South Atlantic.

crew and ask if there was anything else they needed, either in Concepción or on San Felix Island. They said that they were very happy with everything so General Rodriguez and I returned to the ramp to watch as refuelling finished and the aircraft prepared for departure.

Shortly afterwards, Nimrod taxied away from the ramp and accelerated down the runway to lift off and head south to begin its first intelligence-gathering flight along the Argentine border and out into the South Atlantic. General Rodriguez and I remained at Concepción to keep in touch via Chilean Air Force secure communications in case of any unforeseen problems with the Nimrod flight. It was always an option for the Nimrod crew to return to Concepción at the end of their mission if necessary to refuel before heading back to San Felix Island. Meanwhile, Captain Perez returned to Santiago, where he had other duties to perform.

Once we received news many hours later that Nimrod had returned safely to San Felix Island, General Rodriguez invited me to a splendid fish restaurant on the coast, where we enjoyed a lovely meal together before returning to the airport at Concepción for the flight back to Santiago. Our aircraft was a small, Chilean Air Force, twin propeller-engined machine with two pilots and six passenger seats in the cabin. It was similar to the aircraft in which we had flown to San Felix Island with Commander Pedro Anguita. Apart from General Rodriguez and me in the passenger cabin, there was a female Chilean Air Force Captain, who needed a lift back to Santiago.

The first part of the flight was uneventful but we soon entered what I realised was an embedded cumulonimbus cloud. The turbulence became extremely severe and we started to be thrown around the sky as if we were performing aerobatics. With only lap straps to hold us in our seats, we three passengers found it difficult to prevent our arms, legs and heads from flailing about. The lady passenger started to scream and was violently sick. The General and I tried to calm her down and tell her that this sort of thing was normal but, as experienced pilots, he and I exchanged glances which we both knew meant that this aircraft was close to breaking up in mid-air and that we had no chance of survival if it did so. Suddenly, the door to the flight deck flew open, due to the extreme aerodynamic forces twisting the airframe. From my seat I could see the instrument panel and noted that the instruments 'were all over the place', while the two pilots were fighting to maintain control of the aircraft. The door then started to swing about, banging loudly and violently between its twisted door frame and the bulkhead, adding to the noise and general confusion. None of us could risk undoing our seat belt to try to secure the door as we could have been seriously injured, so the door continued to do its own thing.

Just as I thought this flight was about to end in disaster, we came out of the worst of the turbulence into what I would describe as merely severe turbulence, then into normal turbulence, shortly followed by relatively gentle conditions. The General and I exchanged looks of relief and the lady stopped screaming, while the aircraft Captain shouted apologies from the front. As we came out of cloud, we could see that we were on the outskirts of Santiago, preparing to land at one of the small military airfields. As the pilots extended the flaps to slow down for landing, the aircraft flipped onto its back. We were hanging upside down in our seats, with arms and legs dangling like rag dolls. Of course, the lady screamed again and I thought that we really were going to die this time. The stresses imposed on the aircraft by the violent air currents in the thundercloud had twisted the wings so much that only one of the wing flaps had extended when the crew selected them. This had caused a violent roll, turning us upside down before the pilots could select the flaps up again to regain control of the aircraft. They gently rolled the aircraft the right way up again and the Captain shouted another apology to us.

Since he would no longer be able to use the flaps for landing, the Captain correctly decided to fly to another airport with a longer runway, where he could land safely at the higher speed needed to land flapless. After a normal flapless landing, we taxied into dispersal. The General, the two pilots and I were then able to inspect the significant amount of damage caused by our flight through the storm. The wings, fuselage and tailplane were visibly warped and we all agreed that the aircraft would not have been able to withstand much more punishment before breaking up in flight. We considered that it had been badly overstressed and was unlikely ever to fly again. We thanked the pilots and congratulated them on their skilful handling of a hazardous situation. Our lady passenger seemed to have regained her composure, as she politely declined the General's offer of a lift to the nearest hospital. However, to avoid putting her off flying for the rest of her life, we changed tack completely from our earlier reassurance in the middle of the storm that this was a perfectly normal flight. We now told her that this had been the worst storm any of us had encountered during four long flying careers, so she was most unlikely to suffer a repeat performance. I have no idea whether this tactic worked or whether she decided to use surface transport thereafter.

Nimrod successfully flew several other missions from San Felix Island, refuelling at night at Concepción. During its high-altitude flights just inside Chilean airspace and then out into the South Atlantic it was able to use its electronic sensors to collect valuable intelligence on Argentine military emissions. Although the Chilean Air Force operated ELINT aircraft, these were small, twin-engined propeller machines that lacked the high-altitude performance needed to 'look over' the Andes and the range needed to fly well out into the South Atlantic.

One night in May, I was asleep in the camp bed in my Embassy office when the Duty Clerk woke me to transfer a telephone call from London. When I asked the Duty Clerk who was on the line he gave me a nickname which told me that it was Ken Hayr. I knew immediately that this was something urgent because, for security reasons, Ken and I did not use the telephone. Soon after my arrival in Santiago, I had sent to Ken by secure signal this nickname and one for me with a one-time code in case we should ever need to contact each other urgently in clear language. Ken was quite agitated and from the code I gathered that our Nimrod had just been intercepted by Chilean Air Force fighters as it re-entered Chilean airspace on returning from its mission into the South Atlantic. It appeared that the Nimrod had been within a whisker of being shot down and Ken naturally wanted to know as soon as possible what had happened and why. I said that I knew nothing about this incident but would investigate and report back as soon as possible.

I telephoned Patricio to tell him that I needed to speak most urgently with General Rodriguez and that this needed to be in a secure environment with secure communication links to other parts of the Chilean Air Force. Patricio said

59

that the General was at home but he would ask him to go to the Chilean Air Force Intelligence HQ where Patricio would take me. By the time I had dressed, Patricio was at the Embassy gates and he drove swiftly through Santiago to the Intelligence HQ, where General Rodriguez had just arrived. We went straight to the General's office and I explained the problem. He immediately picked up his secure telephone link to the radar station at Punta Arenas and spoke to the Senior Duty Officer there. When he put the telephone down, General Rodriguez apologized profusely to me and explained what had happened.

In order to reduce the risk of a security leak, the Base Commander at Punta Arenas had decided to limit the knowledge of Nimrod operations to himself and the Senior Duty Officer of each shift. Unfortunately, this officer was down the corridor taking a break at the time Nimrod appeared on the radar screen entering Chilean airspace on returning from its mission into the South Atlantic. Since it was an unidentified intruder and the only person who could have verified that this was a friendly aircraft was not available, they scrambled a Chilean Air Force fighter aircraft from Punta Arenas to intercept it. The Nimrod crew detected this fast-moving radar plot chasing them and attempted to evade the fighter by applying full power and diving to increase speed, hoping to outrun the fighter. This made the Chileans even more suspicious of the intruder and they were seriously discussing whether to shoot it down as soon as they got within firing range. Luckily, the Senior Duty Officer reappeared just in time to call off the interception.

Thus, we narrowly avoided the loss of one of our most important assets, including the tragic and unnecessary deaths of all aircrew on board. In addition, losing Nimrod in this way would almost certainly have put an end to all of our clandestine operations with Chile, which in turn would probably have caused us to lose the war. Incidents like this happen in all wars but I hoped at the time that this would be the last in Chile. This demonstrated to General Rodriguez and me the downside of applying the 'need-to-know' principle too assiduously and we resolved immediately to ask the Base Commander at Punta Arenas to ensure that, when Nimrod was airborne, there was always at least one officer at his desk at all times who knew about the Nimrod operations. We had no more incidents of this type but it had been a very near thing.

I immediately returned to the Embassy to report by signal to Ken Hayr with a full explanation of what had happened and why. I was also able to reassure Ken that there would be no more such incidents. I later discovered that our Nimrod Captain and his crew thought at the time that it was an Argentine fighter with orders to shoot Nimrod down. This is why they tried so hard to escape and there were certainly some very anxious moments on board our aircraft until what they thought was an enemy aircraft abandoned the chase.

It was at this stage that I received a very pleasant surprise. A signal arrived from Ken Hayr to inform me that my promotion to Group Captain had just come through. He congratulated me on my promotion and said that he had telephoned Patricia at home to give her the good news.

Shortly afterwards, the British nuclear-powered submarine HMS *Conqueror* sank the Argentine cruiser *Belgrano*. This proved to be a crucial and controversial event. It was crucial because thereafter the Argentine surface fleet was forced to remain within their territorial waters to avoid attack from our submarines. This powerful force was thus effectively neutralised for the remainder of the war and no longer threatened our Task Force. Had the *Belgrano*, which outgunned all of our surface ships, and the *25 de Mayo*, the Argentine aircraft carrier, together with the many other warships in the Argentine fleet, been free to attack the British Task Force at will it is unlikely that we would have been able to recapture the Falklands.

However, the sinking of the *Belgrano* with the sad loss of 321 Argentine lives was controversial because the warship was outside the Total Exclusion Zone when it was attacked. Intelligence gained from intercepts of Argentine signals at the time showed that the Argentine Navy was preparing to mount a two-pronged attack on the British Task Force. It could be argued that the pre-emptive strike by HMS *Conqueror* prevented a fierce naval battle which would have resulted in the loss of many ships on both sides and a much larger loss of life than occurred when the *Belgrano* sank. There can be no doubt that, from a purely military point of view, the sinking of the *Belgrano* was fully justified.

I considered this event to signal the moment when the 'real war' started and my life became even more hectic from this moment on. The revenge attack two days later, when a Super Etendard aircraft of the Argentine Navy sank the British warship HMS *Sheffield* with an Exocet missile, confirmed that the gloves were now off.

Chapter 8

My office/bedroom telephone awoke me at about 2 a.m.
It was Patricio asking me to be ready for him to collect
me from the Embassy to meet General Rodriguez, who
needed to see me urgently. Within 30 minutes we were
in the General's office. He was extremely agitated as he
explained that the burnt-out remains of a British military
helicopter had been discovered in southern Chile. He
needed to know urgently what was going on because he
and General Matthei were 'getting a lot of flack' from
General Pinochet, who wanted to know what a British
helicopter was doing in Chile. I explained truthfully that
I had no idea about this incident but would make urgent
enquiries and report back to General Rodriguez as soon
as possible.

I explained that it would help my enquiries if he would
tell me everything he knew about this incident, such as
the type of helicopter, exactly where it had been found,
the extent of the damage, whether it appeared to have
crashed, whether there was any sign of damage from enemy
action and what had happened to the crew. The General
told me that it was a Royal Naval Sea King helicopter,
that it did not appear to have crashed but seemed to have
been deliberately set on fire. It had been found not far
from Punta Arenas and there was no sign of the crew.
He added that the Chilean armed forces and Carabiñeros
were carrying out extensive searches in the local area to

Sea King Helicopter. A version of this helicopter was used on a one-way mission to insert an SAS patrol in southern Argentina. It then flew across the border into Chile, where it was set on fire and abandoned.

try to find the crew. He promised to inform me immediately if they located the crew or discovered anything else significant about this incident. Meanwhile, they were of course guarding the wreckage.

General Rodriguez then asked me what I thought may have happened and why my authorities had not informed me about this mission, so that I could in turn have tipped him off. I told him that it might have been an aborted reconnaissance mission. I repeated that I had not been informed and said this was probably because, under our need-to-know principle, only those directly involved would have been informed, to avoid the risk of compromising the mission. I apologised to General Rodriguez and asked him to pass on my apologies to Generals Matthei and Pinochet, adding that I realised what an embarrassing and difficult situation this had caused for them and their country. I promised to give them the full story as soon as possible and said that I would do my best to minimise the impact of this event.

Patricio then drove me back to the Embassy. On the way, I tried to think what this mission might have been and what could have gone wrong. I thought it was probably a Special Forces mission into southern Argentina that had gone wrong in some way. This would explain why the crew had set fire to their helicopter and gone into hiding. Their instructions in circumstances such as this would have been to escape and evade capture for as long as possible in order to protect the Special Forces they had dropped the other side of the border. I did not think that Ken Hayr would have been informed because this seemed to have been a local, tactical operation that, under the same need-to-know basis, did not involve him. However, I hoped I would soon discover what had happened because this incident had suddenly presented me with insuperable difficulties over future cooperation with my Chilean colleagues. For the first time since I had arrived in Chile, I felt that there was a serious danger that the incredible mutual trust that the Chileans and I had rapidly established was in serious jeopardy.

On arrival at the Embassy, I immediately drafted an urgent signal to Ken, explaining what had happened at this end and asking what I could tell the Chileans. I asked Patricio to wait because I thought that I would have an answer quite soon and would therefore need to go back to see General Rodriguez. I did not have to wait very long for Ken Hayr's reply. He said that he did not know in advance about this operation and he could not give me any details even now. However, he gave me a line to take with my Chilean hosts that might ease the situation. I was to describe this as a routine reconnaissance mission that experienced a serious failure in its navigation equipment and a complete loss of communication. This caused the crew to become lost in extremely bad weather. When they were running out of fuel they had no alternative but to land at the first suitable spot. Believing that they were probably in Argentina, they carried out standard procedure in such circumstances, which was to destroy their helicopter and attempt to escape.

Patricio and I returned to General Rodriguez and I repeated Ken's explanation. I had no idea whether the General believed the story but he seemed genuinely relieved to have some information. He immediately used his secure telephone to call General Matthei and when he had finished told me that General Matthei was grateful for my information. He then told me that news of this helicopter incident was now circulating widely in the world's media, with many reporters and camera crews now converging on the area. General Rodriguez added that they would continue to search for the crew and let me know as soon as they had any news.

Chilean newspapers and television screens were soon reporting extensively on the story, showing images of the helicopter wreckage as reporters tried to explain what they thought might have happened. As usual following such events, their coverage was very short on facts but full of wild speculation. Of course, it was in our interest for this story to fade rapidly from the headlines but one reporter was particularly persistent in keeping the story alive. He continued to pop up on television screens with images of the burnt-out helicopter wreckage in the background, spouting increasingly wild theories.

I remarked casually to Patricio that I would be pleased when this particular man decided to turn his attention to something less damaging to our cause. Sure enough, a short time after my conversation, this man's coverage suddenly stopped. When I asked Patricio what had happened to this reporter, he smiled and said: 'Don't worry, he's still alive and well but very scared! He won't be reporting on the helicopter any more!' Apparently, following my remark to Patricio, two very large and ugly men in civilian clothes had visited this reporter in his hotel bedroom. They showed him that they were armed and spoke very intently. They explained that if he did not leave the area immediately, they could not guarantee his safety. They also told him that if he ever spoke about their visit or the conversation, he would regret it because they had ways of finding him wherever he was in Chile or elsewhere. When he asked how he could explain to his colleagues, friends and family why he was suddenly leaving, his visitors told him to think up a good story because he had plenty of practice at that. I felt very sorry for this reporter but, although I did not approve of the method, I was certainly pleased with the result because he did not appear any more reporting on the helicopter story and it soon faded from the headlines for a while.

However, this was by no means the end of the story for General Rodriguez and me. A few days later, he told me that the Sea King crew had turned themselves in at a Carabiñeros post near Punta Arenas. They were apparently very cold and hungry but otherwise safe and well. Apart from admitting that they were indeed the missing crew of the Sea King helicopter, they were saying nothing about their mission, what had happened to them or why they were in Chile. I asked General Rodriguez if he would kindly keep the lid on this news, transfer the men to Chilean Air Force care and fly them up to Santiago for me to look after, before I could arrange to get them out of the country quietly. He agreed but said that I should make no firm arrangements for them to leave the country before he had the opportunity to speak to General Matthei.

On returning to the Embassy, I passed this news by urgent signal to Ken Hayr and informed the Ambassador, John Heath, and the Consul, John Cummins. We spent some time discussing the implications. We agreed that if possible we should get the crew out of Chile and back to the UK discreetly. However, we also felt that we should have a back-up plan in case news of the crew's discovery leaked. If there was a leak, we realised that there would be a somewhat complicated process involved whereby the Chilean Ministry of Foreign Affairs and military junta in Santiago, the British Foreign Office and Ministry of Defence in London, and the Ambassador in Santiago would all have to agree what should happen to the crew. Meanwhile, we put plan A into effect.

It would obviously not be a good idea to arrange accommodation for the crew in a Santiago hotel. Equally, although John Heath and John Cummins would have been happy to accommodate them, their houses would be among the first places that reporters would look if the story broke. We therefore asked Alison, the secretary to Head of Chancery, Robert Gordon, if she would kindly move into a hotel for a few days so that we could lodge the crew in her apartment. Alison readily agreed and there would be no leaks from her because she had a very high security clearance for her work.

As part of my contingency planning when I first arrived in Santiago, I had already stored a quantity of civilian clothing and shoes in my office in case any British military personnel arrived in Chile in uniform. I had begged these items from Embassy colleagues, including the Ambassador, explaining to them that what would no longer be suitable for a diplomat to wear, would be more than adequate for one of my 'refugees' to wear for a few days. I therefore had an assortment of shapes and sizes available, so I thought that I would be able to clothe this helicopter crew suitably. A few hours later, the Captain of the Sea King helicopter, Lieutenant Hutchings of the Royal Marines, and his two fellow crew members were safely installed in Alison's apartment in Santiago. They looked suitably nondescript dressed in their borrowed clothing. Indeed, the man for whom one of the Ambassador's cast-off suits had proved to be a very good fit, swore that he would continue to wear it for best when he returned to the UK because it was better than anything he owned at home!

There followed a short period of intense discussion about how and when we would fly our unexpected guests out of Chile. This discussion involved a great deal of signals traffic between the Foreign Office and the Ambassador on the one hand and the Ministry of Defence and me on the other. It also meant many visits for the Ambassador to the Ministry of Foreign Affairs in Santiago as well as for me to visit Generals Matthei and Rodriguez. It was eventually agreed by all parties that it would be better to come clean about the discovery of the helicopter crew, to hold a press conference and then fly them out of the country openly. If handled carefully, this would avoid any suggestion that the Chileans were cooperating with the British armed forces by allowing aircraft to operate in Chilean airspace. It would also scotch any rumours that the helicopter crew might have been badly treated when they were found.

So that the Ambassador and Consul could speak to Lt Hutchings and his crew to ensure that they were well prepared for a press conference, Patricio and I took them very late one night to the Ambassador's house, which was some way from the Embassy. We arrived in Patricio's car and held a very successful meeting. However, just as we were preparing to leave, several reporters and camera crews appeared at the front of the house. It appeared that there had either been a leak or else someone had jumped the gun on releasing news of the discovery of the crew. Whatever the reason, we certainly did not want the crew to face the press yet so the Ambassador's wife kindly volunteered to guide us through the extensive back garden in pitch darkness so that we could climb over a back wall and escape on foot via a quiet street. This would allow Mr Heath and John Cummins to create a diversion at the front of the house, pretending to say an extended farewell to each other at the front entrance. Of course, Patricio's car had to be left at the front of the house but he could recover it later.

Mrs Heath was obviously enjoying her role supporting her husband in this episode. We did not want to use torches for fear of drawing the attention of the waiting press, so it proved quite tricky negotiating the various obstacles in the back garden. Without her detailed knowledge of the garden's layout, we would have been in serious trouble. At one stage, Mrs Heath whispered to us to be careful not to fall into the swimming pool because it had been emptied for cleaning, so we risked injury rather than a soaking. We eventually reached the far wall with no mishaps and, with a whispered thank you and goodbye to Mrs Heath, we went over the wall and walked away. Patricio soon located a public telephone and called a colleague to collect us so that we could return Lt Hutchings and his crew to Alison's apartment.

The next day there was full media coverage of the

discovery of the Sea King crew and details of a press conference to be held the next day in the British Embassy. There was also news that the British Ambassador had been summoned to the Ministry of Foreign Affairs to receive an official protest about an illegal and unjust infringement of Chilean airspace by the British military helicopter. So far, everything was going to plan and in due course, Mr Heath went to the Ministry of Foreign Affairs to receive the official protest and to offer his apologies for this mishap.

The press conference took place in the ground floor reception area of the British Embassy. Lt Hutchings and his crew were sitting behind a desk and the remainder of the room was crowded with reporters and camera crews. John Cummins and I were also behind the desk but hidden from public view behind a wall. Lt Hutchings spoke in English, reading from a prepared statement. He said that he had been on a routine reconnaissance mission when his aircraft suffered a serious equipment failure in very bad weather conditions. This caused a complete loss of his navigation and communications equipment so that he became uncertain of his position and was unable to contact anyone to inform them of his problems. He continued flying, whilst trying to locate his position, until his fuel tanks were almost empty. Eventually he had to land at the first suitable spot before lack of fuel caused him to crash. After landing, believing that he was almost certainly in Argentina, he decided to destroy his helicopter to avoid it falling into enemy hands. He and his crew then moved well away from the helicopter and went into hiding to avoid capture. This was standard practice in such circumstances. Eventually, lack of food and adverse weather forced them to give themselves up and they then realised that they had inadvertently crossed the border into Chile. Hutchings added that they apologised for illegally entering the country, had been treated very well by the Chilean authorities and were most grateful for the help they had been given. He finished by saying that copies of his statement in English and Spanish would be available afterwards but he regretted that neither he nor his crew could answer any questions. Although I knew that this story was about as far from the truth as it could possibly be, the media reported it in good faith and no stories appeared offering alternative theories.

After the war, my wife told me that she had watched this press conference on the television news in England. She was apparently convinced that I was involved and even thought she caught a glimpse of me ushering the crew from the room at the end. In fact, this was the Consul, John Cummins, who emerged from behind the wall to escort the crew away. I was very careful to remain hidden from view. John and I were of similar height, build and hair colour, so I understood how Patricia could have made this assumption. The following day, Lt Hutchings and his crew flew back to the UK, avoiding any publicity. As I saw them boarding their aircraft, I was particularly amused to see the man who was wearing the Ambassador's donated suit looking extremely smart as he climbed the aircraft steps. I imagined that he would probably wear that suit to weddings, funerals and other special occasions for some years to come.

Chapter 9

Other matters of much more interest to the world's media replaced the Sea King helicopter story in the headlines. As far as General Rodriguez and I were concerned, this was ideal because we now had a most important and difficult matter to resolve. We definitely did not want any publicity this time. Ken Hayr authorised me to tell General Rodriguez in the strictest confidence the true nature of the helicopter incident. The Sea King was engaged on an extremely daring and secret mission. The machine had been stripped of all non-essential equipment and fittings so that it could carry a maximum fuel load plus eight members of the SAS with all their weapons, ammunition and equipment. This was a one-way mission to drop these Special Forces in southern Argentina before the crew flew across the border to Chile. Once there, they were to ditch their helicopter in the sea and hide until the SAS patrol had finished their mission. I explained to General Rodriguez that, for security reasons and to protect the patrol, the nature of the mission was known only to those who needed to know: this certainly did not include the helicopter crew, me or anyone else in Chile. General Rodriguez fully understood and accepted this but said that it was a pity because, had he known about it in advance, the crew would not have needed to destroy their helicopter. He said that we could have hushed the whole thing up and refuelled the helicopter so that the crew could have flown it back to the Task Force at night.

However, General Rodriguez was not one to dwell on what might have been and he now promised me every possible help to resolve the current problem as quickly as possible but with maximum security. I explained that the patrol was now in hiding on the Chilean side of the border and we would like to move them up to the Santiago area in complete secrecy and hide them where they could recover from their mission. They could then either be flown discreetly back to the UK or, equally discreetly, re-inserted across the border into Argentina, depending on British military requirements. As I had come to expect, General Rodriguez moved with alacrity. The SAS patrol was soon extracted from its position in southern Chile to be flown back at night to a Chilean Air Force Base near Santiago. The pilot who flew them back was a highly trusted ex-Chilean Air Force pilot who was often used by Chilean Air Force Intelligence for clandestine work. He was flying a twin turbo-prop passenger aircraft on a civil registration. The pilot flew his aircraft back to Punta Arenas the next day with his wife, nanny and children as passengers. En route, this aircraft disappeared over southern Chile and sadly no trace could be found of either the aircraft or its occupants. Whilst any death is very sad, I consider this to have been perhaps the most tragic loss of life during the Falklands War.

Patricio and I collected the SAS men in an unmarked vehicle to take them and their equipment to a Chilean Air Force Intelligence safe house. This was a large log cabin in an extensive wooded area near Santiago. It had log fires, several rooms, bathrooms, a kitchen and extensive grounds. The men were very happy to be in such comfortable surroundings after their time living rough in adverse weather. They were able to clean and dry their clothing and equipment here. They also enjoyed some good food and used the extensive grounds to exercise and keep themselves fully fit for action again.

In the event, I later received instructions that this patrol should be flown back to the UK. General Rodriguez kindly chartered a civilian-registered Boeing 707 aircraft on my behalf. This was also flown by a highly trusted ex-Chilean Air Force crew that carried out work for Chilean Air Force Intelligence. The patrol was thus spirited out of Chile with no leaks to the media. I never heard the official story behind this incident but, after the war, I was able to make quite a good guess at their likely mission, based on various pieces of information that leaked into the public domain. I therefore came to the following conclusion.

The Argentine Exocet missiles were such a serious threat to our Task Force that the top priority was to eliminate them by any available means. Since, for political reasons, the British War Cabinet had ruled out bombing or missile attacks against mainland Argentina, the only alternative was to mount a Special Forces operation against the base in southern Argentina from which aircraft carrying Exocet were launched. The intention of such an attack would be to destroy the missiles themselves, the Super Etendard aircraft that carried them, the pilots who flew them or even all three. Such a mission carried enormous risks, would require a large number of Special Forces and extremely accurate, up-to-date intelligence. Otherwise, the attacking force could arrive to find that the aircraft, missiles and crews had just moved to another location.

Approximately 100 Special Forces men would need to fly in at night and under radar cover to land on the enemy runway. Two C130 Hercules transport aircraft would be required for this mission and it would be a prerequisite that a Special Forces patrol, inserted by a Sea King helicopter, would already be observing the base clandestinely to give their colleagues up-to-date information and, if necessary, call the operation off at the last minute. This reconnaissance patrol would also be able to create a diversion to help the invading force and/or assist the survivors of the main force to escape if the C130 Hercules aircraft were destroyed or damaged and unable to take off again. This plan was the subject of intense discussion in London, in the Task Force and indeed within the Special Forces. Some considered it a suicide mission but others thought it was just the sort of operation for which British Special Forces had become renowned and which might well work because it was such a bold and unexpected move.

Although it got to an advanced stage of planning, this assault was finally abandoned. The degree to which planning had advanced is shown by the fact that the Sea King helicopter had already delivered the Special Forces patrol when the operation was called off. There appear to have been several reasons for this 'no-go' decision. First, there was strong political pressure to avoid attacking mainland Argentina. It was considered that this would have alienated many of the countries, particularly in South America, that supported our decision to recover the Falklands but would have considered attacks on mainland Argentina to be a step too far. Then, the discovery of the Sea King helicopter in Chile had partly lifted the lid on the operation and had probably warned Argentina that something was afoot. Also, by now Argentina had already used most of the few remaining Exocet missiles. As is so often the case in a fast-moving combat situation, new factors had caused the balance of risk to swing towards not carrying out this mission. The benefits achieved if the attack were successful no longer justified the risks involved.

Chapter 10

Soon after the initial shock of the invasion, it became apparent in the MOD in London and in the Joint Force HQ at Northwood that we were extremely short of up-to-date, accurate intelligence on the disposition of the Argentine armed forces. In particular, there was no high-altitude photo-reconnaissance (PR) capability available to the Task Force. Since the early days of aerial warfare during World War I, we had always relied on good PR when planning military operations. PR developed to a quite astonishing degree during World War II and it continued to improve thereafter. It was therefore not surprising that Ken Hayr should enlist my help in attempting to do something about this gap in our capability. At the time, the Royal Air Force was using Canberra aircraft for high-

Canberra Aircraft. RAF crews flew Photographic Reconnaissance versions of this aircraft to Belize in Central America, where they were held in reserve during the war.

altitude PR. This was a variant of the twin-engined jet bomber, which had been in service with the RAF for over 30 years. The Canberra was also sold to many other air forces around the world, ironically including the Argentine Air Force, which was using them against British forces in the Falklands War.

I asked General Matthei if he would allow us to base some RAF PR Canberras in Chile so that we could mount reconnaissance sorties to gain up-to-date intelligence on the disposition of Argentine armed forces. I explained that, flying at very high altitude in Chilean and international airspace, using their oblique cameras, our Canberras could bring back very high-resolution photos of items of military interest in Argentina. General Matthei said that he was familiar with the Canberra's qualities and thought that our two countries could benefit from having access to this sort of information. However, he felt that the Canberra was such a distinctive aircraft that we would not be able to keep its presence in Chile a secret. He explained that the Chilean Air Force had previously wanted to buy some Canberras from the UK but that for political reasons the British Government of the day had not authorised this. He suggested that if we were now prepared to sell Chile some at an acceptable price, the sale could be portrayed as a normal part of Chile's defence procurement. Obviously, some RAF air and ground crews would be needed initially to train their Chilean Air Force counterparts to operate the Canberra. General Matthei thought that there could be no better way of carrying out this training than to mount the sort of reconnaissance sorties I had described!

General Matthei's reasoning was sound and I agreed to pass his suggestion back to the UK. Within a few days, this plan was accepted with one proviso. For valid intelligence

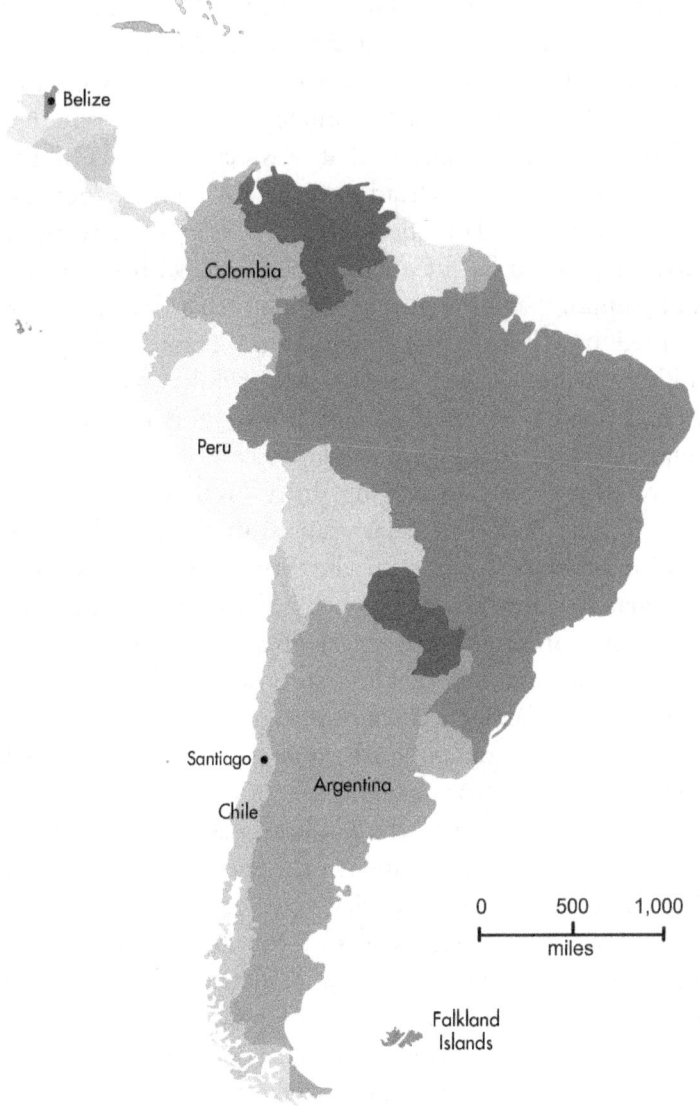

Canberra aircraft were flown to Belize to await deployment to Chile.

reasons, the UK MOD did not want news of the sale to be released before the Canberras were able to carry out their first few reconnaissance sorties. It was hoped that this would enable valuable intelligence to be obtained before Argentina realised what was happening. On this basis, the deal went ahead and an RAF C130 Hercules transport aircraft later flew to Easter Island, carrying an advance party of RAF Canberra specialists, with spare parts and support equipment. Overnight, this Hercules was painted in Chilean Air Force colours before flying to a military airfield outside Santiago. Meanwhile, two Canberras were prepared in the UK and flown to Belize to await final clearance to fly into Chile.

Following this encouraging flurry of activity, there was a frustrating period of delays caused by both Chilean and British procrastination. On the British side, the sceptics felt that the presence of Canberra aircraft would be easily detected soon after their arrival in Chile. There were also expressions of doubt that the story about Chile's sudden purchase of Canberra aircraft would be believed, leading to increased tension in South America. Some worried that the unarmed Canberras might be shot down as they carried out their missions. On the Chilean side, although it was agreed that an announcement of the Canberra sale would be delayed until after the first few reconnaissance sorties had been flown, there was still considerable worry that news would leak prematurely and that this would in turn lead to speculation about an Anglo-Chilean military alliance.

To complicate matters further, there was a conflict of interest in the discussions as to where the Canberras should be based. Because these aircraft were not equipped to refuel in the air, the British wanted them to be based as far south as possible in Chile to give them maximum range and endurance while carrying out their reconnaissance missions. The Chileans, on the other hand, preferred an airfield further north, where they believed they could more easily keep these operations secret. In the end, two events intervened to decide matters.

First of all, a story appeared in the media that RAF Phantom fighter aircraft had flown to Punta Arenas, where they were to be based for operations against Argentine forces. This was complete fabrication and may even have been misinformation planted by Argentina. The truth was that Phantoms had indeed left the UK but had flown to Ascension Island rather than to Punta Arenas. It had been decided that Ascension Island needed some air defence capability in case Argentina decided to mount attacks on this important British base. The Phantoms based on Ascension would also be ready to help with air cover for the British Task Force and forces ashore on the Falklands if they could in due course be deployed to an airbase ashore.

RAF Phantom Aircraft were sent to Ascension Island in the Atlantic to provide air defence against possible Argentine air attack.

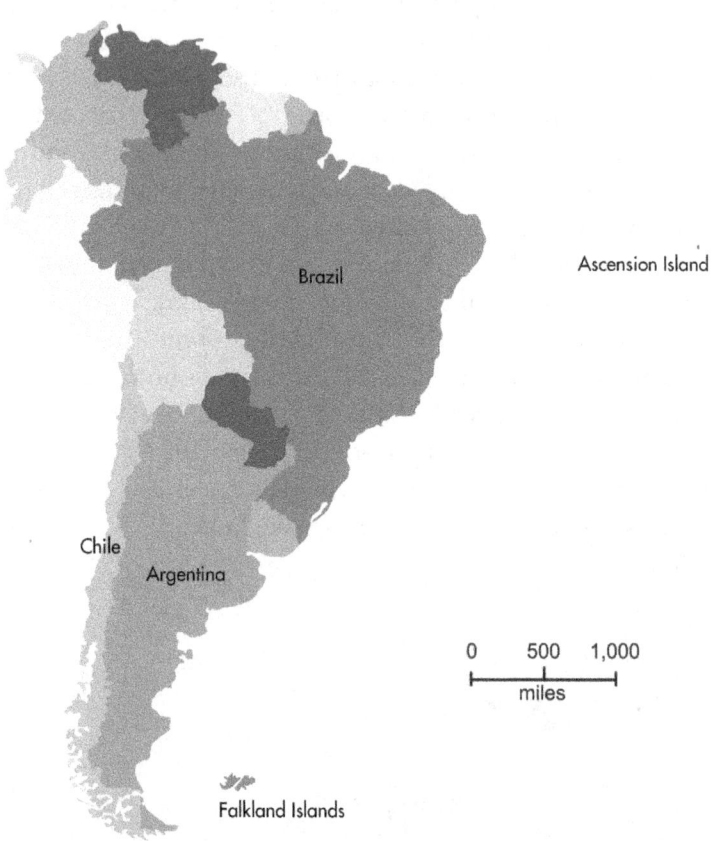

Approximately midway between the UK and the Falkland Islands, Ascension Island was the main staging post for British forces throughout the war.

This unfortunate story caused the Chileans and British to delay further the decision to fly the Canberras into Chile and they continued to be held in reserve in Belize. Next, delays in deploying the Canberras to Chile meant that other methods of obtaining up-to-date intelligence about Argentine military deployments had to be used. There was thus now less urgency to use the Canberras and it was eventually agreed that the RAF C130 Hercules and its load of men and material should return to the UK. The Canberras also left Belize to return to the UK.

However, this was not an entirely wasted exercise because, shortly after the war ended, the deal went through as planned and the Chilean Air Force was successfully operating Canberras later in 1982. Unfortunately, one of these aircraft was lost in a flying accident, although the two aircrew escaped. It seems that this aircraft was on a routine training mission, flying in conditions of strong air turbulence. The pilot was suddenly ejected involuntarily and the navigator had no alternative but to eject also because he was occupying his own seat in a separate part of the aircraft with no access to the flying controls. This accident appears to have been caused by a servicing error, whereby the bottom latch of the pilot's ejector seat had not been correctly secured so that the seat rode up its positioning rail due to the strong turbulence, thus firing the seat ejection mechanism. With nobody to fly it, the Canberra crashed but fortunately the aircrew survived and nobody on the ground was killed or injured.

Chapter 11

From the start of my time in Chile, Punta Arenas proved to be a very important place. It was much closer to the war zone, as well as to key Argentine airfields and ports, than Santiago and was therefore where we obtained a great deal of vital intelligence about the Argentine forces. I made several visits to the area, usually travelling on a scheduled flight by LADECO, one of the two Chilean National Airlines. The flight normally took about three hours. On my first visit soon after arriving in Santiago, I found that Punta Arenas was already on a strict war footing. As soon as the aircraft started descending for its approach to the airport, all blinds in the passenger cabin were closed and had to remain closed until passengers left the aircraft after landing. The vigilant cabin crew prevented any attempts by passengers to raise the blinds slightly to peep outside or even worse to take photos. On departure the window blinds were closed before passengers boarded the aircraft and remained closed until the aircraft reached cruising altitude.

At night, airfield lighting was on only when aircraft were taking off or landing. At all other times a strict blackout was imposed. The airfield was well protected by anti-aircraft gun and missile defences, with armed fighter aircraft on standby to scramble against any attacks. All Chilean Air Force personnel were fully armed and wearing combat dress and steel helmets. From all of this, it was

Punta Arenas, the most southerly town in Chile, where vital intelligence was gathered and passed to the British Task Force during the war.

evident that the Chileans expected an attack from Argentina and were fully prepared to defend themselves.

Situated on the northern shore of the Straits of Magellan, Punta Arenas at the time had a population of about 100,000. It had a distinctly frontier atmosphere, with many buildings made of wood or metal and painted in bright colours. At the time of my visits, it was always very cold with strong winds blowing and frequent storms. During one visit with General Rodriguez, we attempted to fly in a helicopter from Punta Arenas to visit a nearby radar site. The General sat in the front with the pilot and I got into the back. The wind was too strong for the pilot to start the engine and engage the rotor safely in the open so he did this just inside the hangar with the downwind doors of the building open. The pilot then taxied into the open but remained in the lee of the hangar to lift off into wind. As we lifted above the shelter of the hangar, the full force of the wind hit us and, even though the pilot applied full power and tilted the machine steeply

86

forward to increase flying speed, we flew backwards over the ground for some distance before moving slowly forwards. The turbulence was extremely strong and our progress over the ground was so slow that it took quite a long time to reach the far side of the airfield. However, the pilot continued towards our destination and I estimated our ground speed to be only about 30 to 40 knots. After about 20 minutes, the machine suddenly turned round and headed back to Punta Arenas. With the wind now behind us, I estimated our ground speed to be nearer 200 knots and we rapidly returned to a position just downwind of the hangar at Punta Arenas. There followed the most amazing piece of flying skill I have ever witnessed as the pilot flew us from conditions of high airspeed in extreme turbulence into almost calm air at hovering speed. He then took us into the hangar entrance before stopping the rotor and turning off the engine. General Rodriguez and I shook the pilot warmly by the hand as we congratulated him on his flying skill. He apologised for having to turn back but explained that after our departure he received a report that the wind speed at the radar station had increased to well above that at Punta Arenas and was by then well outside safe limits. In the circumstances, I considered this pilot to have been skilful and brave but by no means foolhardy.

On a separate visit to Punta Arenas, I flew in a Chilean Air Force Twin Otter aircraft to inspect possible sites for the portable radar we had sent to Chile to improve radar cover over southern Argentina. We were flying into the Chilean part of Tierra del Fuego and our route took us close to the Argentine town of Ushuaia, which had an important port and airfield. I spent some time on the outward and inbound flights studying Ushuaia through binoculars. I thought that it had much in common with Punta Arenas but I experienced a strange feeling as I watched Ushuaia drift by, thinking that I was now as close as I was ever likely to get to men who were determined to do as much damage as possible to my colleagues in the British armed forces. I read later that the Argentine military hated the fact that the Chilean Air Force could fly so close to Ushuaia with impunity because the border was very near to the town, whereas the Argentine Air Force could not fly close to Punta Arenas, due to its location well inside the Chilean border.

Ushuaia, an important naval and air base in the extreme south of Argentina.

On another occasion, I flew down to Punta Arenas with Patricio and one of the SAS men from our intelligence unit in Santiago. Our mission was to buy a Gemini-type inflatable boat, outboard motors, paddles and associated equipment. Our cover story was that we intended to use our boat for exploring the region, as well as for camping and fishing trips. We looked at several boats and motors, tried some out, haggled about the prices and insisted that some of the equipment was included in the price. Finally, we selected a suitable package and negotiated a discount for cash. Overall, we tried our best to appear like a normal bunch of chaps buying a boat for pleasure trips. Although we did not know, nor did we need to know, the reason for this purchase, we knew that very little camping or fishing would be involved in any time this boat might spend working for Her Majesty's Government. The important thing was that, if it later appeared on an Argentine beach or up an Argentine river, it would not be traceable to the British military.

Chapter 12

On 14 June, when news came to the British Embassy in Santiago that Argentine forces on the Falkland Islands had surrendered, there was a great deal of cheering, hugging, kissing, handshaking and general jubilation. We had all worked extremely long hours with few breaks and were feeling quite exhausted. However, the exhilaration gave us renewed energy and several improvised, short-notice parties took place. One memorable event was when a group of us took a convoy of vehicles into the wooded foothills of the Andes outside Santiago. Our destination was a large log cabin containing a nightclub called Las Brujas (The Witches). There was food, drink, music and dancing until the small hours of the next morning. Many of our Chilean colleagues joined us there and they seemed as pleased as we were with the British victory. This was because success for Argentina in the Falklands would almost certainly have resulted in swarms of Argentine troops crossing the border into Chile. The party at Las Brujas proved to be most enjoyable and when I finally returned to my camp bed at the Embassy, I immediately fell into a wonderfully deep and uninterrupted sleep – the best I had managed since arriving in Santiago in mid-April.

The following weekend was my first break in many weeks and I decided to head for the Pacific coast with some colleagues. We drove to Viña del Mar, about two hours by road from Santiago, and checked into a hotel overlooking the sea. Although it was by then winter in Chile, we were lucky with the weather and were able to walk on the beach, watch birds diving into the sea to resurface with fish in their beaks, and saw hundreds of seals basking on the rocks just offshore. There were also squadrons of pelicans flying very low along the wave crests, using the up-currents of wind to give them lift so that they rarely needed to flap their wings. We had several excellent meals of fish and other high-quality seafood. It appeared so fresh that we joked that the chef had probably just caught it using a rod from the back window of the kitchen. A visit to the nearby port of Valparaiso and an evening spent in the casino at Viña del Mar ensured that we did not waste any of our time on this lovely part of the Chilean coast.

Back at the Embassy on the Monday morning, I found a signal from Ken Hayr summoning me back to London

Viña del Mar, a resort on the Pacific coast near Santiago, where British Embassy staff relaxed after the war.

for a de-briefing. He told me that I would also be able to take a spot of leave to renew my acquaintance with Patricia! Wing Commander Ian Reilly had recently arrived in Santiago and was to deputise for me while I was away. Before the war ended, Ken had decided that I needed help and selected Ian for the task. Ian and I had served together in the early 1970s, flying the Gnat aircraft on the Central Flying School detachment at RAF Kemble in Gloucestershire. He was also a Jaguar fighter pilot who had previously flown in Ecuador with their Air Force, to whom we had sold Jaguars. Ian spoke fluent Spanish and had relevant operational experience, so he was an ideal choice to keep the pot boiling while I was away.

I returned to England for a wonderful reunion with Patricia and a most interesting series of meetings at the MOD in London. Ken Hayr congratulated me and thanked me for the work I had done in Chile. He told me that all of the top brass wanted to see me to thank me personally for what I had done. He also told me in strict confidence that I would receive an OBE for my work but that, to avoid drawing attention to the link with Chile, it would not be awarded in the Falklands War List. He thought people might assume that I had earned the award for my work in MOD Defence Sales but he assured me that the Queen, Prime Minister and senior officers in the MOD were fully aware of the real reason for the award. Indeed, when I attended my investiture at Buckingham Palace in 1983, it was apparent from her conversation with me that Her Majesty was fully aware of the reason for my award. She thanked me very much for my work in Chile during the war and asked me how I was getting on there now. She added that Prince Philip and she had enjoyed their own visit to the country some years before, and Her

Majesty seemed genuinely pleased to be pinning the medal on my chest.

Ken then explained that, after my de-briefing and some leave, I was to return to Santiago to continue my work with the Chilean armed forces. He said that because Argentina had surrendered in the Falklands without agreeing to an overall ceasefire, we could not be sure that they would not attack the Falklands again. It was therefore in our interest to help Chile to become stronger militarily and at the same time to develop further our intelligence capability against Argentina. Ken said that it was approved at the highest level that I should return to Chile for a normal tour of duty, find somewhere to live and take my wife with me. He also asked me to think of a suitable job title but said that this should not be Air Attaché. This title was considered too restricting, bearing in mind the activities in which I would be involved. Ken's final comment to me was that he and I would have a wonderful story to tell in thirty years' time, when classified information about the Falklands War would be released.

The Chief of Air Staff (CAS), Air Chief Marshal Sir Michael Beetham, greeted me like a returning hero. He repeated most of what Ken Hayr had said and told me that, apart from my vital work to help win the war, I had worked wonders for Anglo-Chilean relations. CAS thought that he would soon invite General Matthei and his wife to the UK as guests of the RAF. He said that my wife and I would of course need to accompany the General and his wife back to the UK on that visit. (True to his word, this is precisely what happened during 1983.) CAS then wished me well in my new posting to Santiago and urged me to enjoy the experience. This was a most impressive interview with Sir Michael. I left his office feeling that the next couple of years would give me an excellent chance to consolidate the important work I had just started in Chile, whilst enjoying life with Patricia in a lovely country with an extremely friendly and hospitable population.

My visit to the office of the Chief of Defence Staff (CDS), Admiral of the Fleet Sir Terence Lewin, was equally memorable. The Personal Staff Officer in his outer office was Air Commodore David Brook, who was on the Entry above mine at the RAF College Cranwell and was my mentor during my first three months there. David made a great fuss of me, said he had followed my recent exploits with pride and emphasised that his boss had become a huge fan of mine. When David showed me into the main office, CDS was if anything more enthusiastic than David had indicated. He appeared almost boyish in his pleasure at seeing me and treated me like an old friend. After thanking me for my work in Chile, Sir Terence took great pleasure in telling me a story about my signals back to the MOD during the war. He explained that he regularly took my signals with him to meetings of the War Cabinet. Since my signals were sent via the Foreign Office communication system they were officially designated as telegrams. CDS had therefore decided to coin the phrase 'Sidgrams' when discussing the contents of my signals with colleagues. On one occasion Mrs Thatcher overheard Sir Terence using this word and thereafter would frequently ask Sir Terence what the latest Sidgram had to say about a particular subject under discussion. He found this amusing and endearing at the time and resolved to tell me about it when he saw me. On a more serious note, he said that the contents of my signals were regularly taken into account during discussions in the War Cabinet, as well as in meetings of the Chiefs of Staff in the MOD, at Joint Force HQ Northwood and in the Task Force. CDS stressed that the system I had arranged with Generals Rodriguez and Matthei to pass early warning of air attacks to the Task Force was crucial to our war effort, had saved many lives and was instrumental in assuring our eventual victory.

I had meetings with various other Department Heads in the MOD over the next few days and was then able to go on a short holiday with Patricia. She was naturally delighted about our posting to Chile and looking forward to meeting my new friends in the Chilean armed forces and at the British Embassy in Santiago. I then flew back to Santiago to continue with my work and find somewhere to live, while Patricia cleared up our affairs and prepared to follow me. In accordance with Ken Hayr's instructions, I invented a title for my role in Chile. I suggested that I should become Training and Sales Liaison Officer (TASLO) at the British Embassy, Santiago, and Ken thought that was ideal. This therefore became my official title. A few weeks later, I collected Patricia from a flight to Santiago and took her to the apartment I had rented on the top floor of a tall block. I had chosen it for its security, its location not very far from the Embassy, and the superb views of the city and snow-capped Andes. Patricia was very happy with my choice and we quickly settled into a fascinating and enjoyable time together in Chile.